TALEISIN'S TALES

By the same authors

Cruising in Seraffyn
Seraffyn's Mediterranean Adventure
Seraffyn's European Adventure
Seraffyn's Oriental Adventure
Self-Sufficient Sailor
Capable Cruiser
Care and Feeding of Sailing Crew
Cost-Conscious Cruiser
Storm Tactics Handbook

By Lin Pardey
Bull Canyon: A Boatbuilder, a Writer and Other Wildlife
(prequel to Taleisin's Tales)

By Larry Pardey
Details of Classic Boat Construction: The Hull

DVDs
Storm Tactics: Companion to Storm Tactics Handbook
Get Ready to Cruise: Offshore Sailing, Part One
Get Ready to Cross Oceans: Offshore Sailing, Part Two
Cruising Has No Limits
Cost Control While You Cruise

Lin's and Larry's Newsletter and Cruising Tips
www.landlpardey.com

Taleisin's Tales

Sailing Towards the Southern Cross

LIN AND LARRY PARDEY

Pardey Publications

Bluelake, California and
Kawau Island, New Zealand

L&L Pardey Publications
120 Monda Way
Bluelake California 95525
USA

Private Bag 906
Kawau Island,
Victoria St. West
Auckland 1142
New Zealand

Library of Congress Cataloging-in-Publication Data
Pardey, Lin.
Taleisin's Tales/Lin and Larry Pardey
p. cm.
1. Taleisin (Cutter) 2. Sailing 3. Travel 4. Adventure
I. Pardey, Larry II. Title

797.1'24-dc20 92-31389 CIP

Book design and composition: **Stephen Horsley**
Editing: **Michelle Elvy**
eBook formatting: **Tim Murphy**

USA distribution:
Paradise Cay Publications
P.O. Box 29
Arcata, California 95518
Tel. (toll free) 1-800-736-4509
Tel. 1-707-822-9063, Fax 1-707-822-9163
www.paracay.com

Trade Distribution: Midpoint Trade Books,

New Zealand Distribution:
Boat Books NZ Ltd.
22 Westhaven Drive
Freemans Bay, Auckland 1010
Tel. 09-358 5691
Email: crew@boatbooks.co.nz

ISBN: 978-1-929214-11-2 Print
ISBN: 978-1-929214-20-4 eBook

Printed in USA

For Lini, our god-daughter,

and Molokeini, our godsend

Contents

INTRODUCTION

"The highlight of our voyage? That's easy," Joyce Lhamon said. "The day we sailed into the lagoon at Truk and anchored in front of the village where Tad and I had been Peace Corp volunteers. Even better, watching the local people when we greeted them in their own language. When they learned I had been their teacher 25 years ago our stay turned into a magical reunion, an experience I was thrilled to share with my children."

"I'd be hard pressed to choose," Beth Leonard said. "The Queen Charlotte Islands are definitely in the top five. When we anchored near some of the oldest, most isolated villages teenagers rowed out to invite us ashore. They were really into their culture, gave us an amazing insight into their lives. Then we sailed to anchorages where we felt the complete wildness of the place, bears feeding along the shore, whales within arm's length of the boat."

Evans Starzinger, Beth's partner, nodded in agreement then listed *Hawk*'s voyages to Iceland and to the southern extremes of New Zealand among his highlights.

We were all together on board *Taleisin*, secured alongside a dock in the quiet elegance of Port Madison, only five miles west of the crushing traffic of Seattle, Washington. We'd met Craig and Kay Compton, the dock's owners, the previous summer when they anchored their 28-foot cutter, *Little Wing*, next to us at Cortez Island 250 miles to the north. "Come and stay at our place when you sail south," they'd insisted. Our friendship blossomed and we took up their offer. Craig and Kay dreamed of setting off on a cruise that lasted longer than a month each summer. Now their dream was gathering traction, fueled by the time they were spending with us and with three other cruising couples who had come to anchor in Port Madison.

Larry had no doubts about his cruising highlight. "Africa, that was absolutely the best – the Bushmen in Namibia were amazing. I loved watching them act out stories about tricking lions into hunting for them." Though I shared his enthusiasm for the seven amazing months we spent wandering through the desert landscapes of the Kalahari, my favorites list started with the time we spent living as part of a Tongan family seconded by getting to know the beauties and hardships of life at Harberton Estancia on the southern shores of Tierra del Fuego.

I climbed out onto *Taleisin*'s deck to close the forehatch against the evening chill. In the cabin beneath my feet the sailing memories continued to flow. Out in the open air a pair of eagles swooped from their tree-top nests in search of food for their growing chicks. The laughter and shouts of a gaggle of children rang out from the sailing school dinghies flitting past our stern. Dozens of houses surrounded this well-protected anchorage; no one would describe it as exotic. But knew I would add it to my inventory of special memories because of the people we encountered in its quiet waters.

As I savored this moment, I was reminded of the concerns I'd had when we launched *Taleisin* more than two decades before. I'd worried that cruising the second time around would be anticlimactic. Our first voyage on 24'4" *Seraffyn* had taken us eastward around the world, and we'd never once ventured south of the equator. Larry tried to quell my concerns, saying our intended route south across the equator then west through the islands of the South Pacific would provide the new experiences I craved. Even so, I'd been concerned the increase in cruising boats that had taken place in the past two decades would mean the islanders we met would no longer see us as special guests, no longer afford us a true glimpse into their lives. And once past those fabled islands, what new destinations could we find to lure us onward?

I guess every cruiser worries that they will not find the romance enjoyed by those who went before. But as I listened to the stories being paraded out to encourage Craig and Kay, I realized that each voyager, even if following the same general route of others before them, finds a different world, different from what we'd found, different from what they expected. Our experiences are varied by our personalities, our approaches to voyaging, our goals, the weather and the people we meet along the way.

After the afternoon's guests departed, Larry and I talked about how our cruising on *Taleisin* led us to destinations far different from those we found during our first voyage. We did find quiet anchorages where we could be completely by ourselves and dive overboard clad only in sun-tan lotion. We did get invited into the daily lives of local people in villages around the world. We met new sailing friends, and then caught up with old ones. We had wondrous sailing, rough sailing, boring sailing, plain sailing, but underlying the whole of *Taleisin*'s voyaging tales was a sense of change. Not only the push for recognition among indigenous people worldwide, but also concern for the environment and awareness of the drain of growing populations on small island nations have become topics of conversation everywhere we voyaged. Now we meet many more cruisers interested in playing an active, if only tiny, part in improving the world they live in.

Then there was the change in us. When we set off cruising in *Seraffyn* in 1968, we'd been comfortable with the idea that home *was* our boat, but home base was Newport Beach where we'd built her. We had planned to wander around until that day when crossing oceans no longer acted as an irresistible lure. Then we'd come back and find a tiny boatyard on the waterfront to settle in and work at an age when other people retired. By the time we set off from Newport Beach on *Taleisin* in 1984, we knew population pressures had made that idea financially impossible. So, though I doubt we analyzed it exactly that way, we set sail feeling homeless. Because of this, our voyage led us into a new adventure, one that included finding a different home base and, with it, all the silken threads that can lead to entrapment.

Taleisin's tale is of a voyage through an ever-changing but still fascinating world. Yet underlying everything are the same themes that ran through our first eleven years of wandering under sail: the thrill of getting to know a new boat, of using the wind to cross oceans; the chance to be completely cut off from shore for a few weeks or months at a time while we re-organized our minds and refueled our energies; the chance to explore new places; the excitement of encountering people we'd be unlikely to meet in a "normal life." But most important of all, it was an opportunity to once again experience the unique bond that comes from depending on each other to be both the catalyst and anchor in an ever-changing life.

I could barely contain my excitement as we waited for our ship's bell to ring eight times. At noon, exactly eighteen years from the moment we'd launched Seraffyn, *our new floating home touched salt water for the very first time.*

CHAPTER ONE

LIVING WITH A GHOST

It was dark and cold as we rowed back towards *Taleisin*. The lights from luxurious homes surrounding our Newport Beach, California anchorage marked the far edges of the water. The faces of Dave and Sue Sprinkle, one of the couples we'd just spent the evening with, disappeared into the night before we were 50 feet from their boat. We heard their hatch slide closed to keep in the warmth created by their diesel cabin heater. I turned towards Larry to share some of my thoughts about our first new cruising encounter – it had been a special night, one filled by new sea stories shared in a safe, quiet anchorage – and my heart took a leap: there, before my eyes, was shadowy *Seraffyn*, sitting quietly, waiting, ready for yet another adventure. I looked a second time and shook my head as the moment passed and *Taleisin* came into focus. Yes, *Taleisin*, with her longer, sleeker sheer line, her sharply raked mast and forward portholes. Larry took the last few strokes with his oars and came to rest alongside her chain-plates. The ghost of little *Seraffyn* seemed to slip away as we climbed on board and rushed below into the luxury of the bigger boat that had now replaced her.

I remember the first time 24'4" *Seraffyn*'s ghost came to call. We'd just finished three and a half years of boatbuilding.[1] Several friends had come by to help us tear down the front of 29'6" *Taleisin*'s building shed. For the very first time, sunlight hit her husky stem and we could stand back more than three feet from her towering hull. Larry and I both stopped to stare at the dream that had slowly and sometimes painfully grown to be a reality.

I think he was the first to say, "I'm glad we added that rub rail, keeps her from looking like *Seraffyn*."

For the first time ever, Taleisin's *fate was in someone else's hands as the boat movers carefully maneuvered her out of the shed.*

But as I walked out of the shed to call the boat movers and confirm their arrival time, I happened to look back and see the graceful arc of the boat's stem and *Seraffyn* appeared before my eyes as if to say, "Don't forget me. I was good enough to be your favorite for eleven years."

Three days later the boat movers, Gil and Harry, arrived with their huge duel-axel low-bed tractor-trailer and miniature red escort truck to begin loading *Taleisin*. We'd all worried about this moment. I'd worried about it from the day we'd chosen to build her in this isolated California canyon, five miles up a winding dirt road where the only level ground was man-made and scarce. Our driveway leading up to the building site was long

1 The story of these years is recounted in *Bull Canyon: A Boatbuilder, a Writer and Other Wildlife.*

and steep. Flat ground extended only ten feet in front of the boat. So the front end of the 60-foot-long rig was almost eight feet below the level of the boat. But Gil and Harry didn't hesitate. They disconnected the trailer from the tractor then used house-lifting jacks and blocks to elevate the front of the trailer until it sat level with *Taleisin*'s cradle. Then things began to look easier. For four hours they worked carefully, methodically, jacking up each corner of *Taleisin*'s cradle until they could slide a pair of dolly wheels under each end. Next they slowly rolled the eight-ton boat and its half-ton cradle forward until it rested on the slide which was built right into the center of the trailer.

Now I relaxed as 7300 hours of our work, almost all of our savings plus four years of scheming and dreaming slid gently forward until it rested on the heavy-duty axles of the trailer built to support a vessel many times *Taleisin*'s weight.

I'd expected to be nervous when we relinquished control of *Taleisin*'s fate to strangers for the first time. But we'd carefully researched our options before hiring this specific crew, and from the moment they arrived we knew they cared about our precious project almost as much as we did. I left them to their work of securing the boat and her spars onto the trailer and continued packing for our move towards the water, though I must admit I stopped a dozen times to run out to the boatyard just to feel involved.

Dark had descended on the canyon by the time *Taleisin* was secured and moved clear of her shed. Two cradles now supported her, the one she'd lived on since she'd been planked and another built from supports set in brackets welded right onto the truck bed. I'd used the last of the food we had in the house. The refrigerator was shut down, the cupboards cleaned out: we planned to move from the stone cottage down to the sea right along with *Taleisin*. So we maneuvered our battered pickup truck carefully past the huge tractor-trailer rig and drove nine miles for our last dinner at the café next to Lake Elsinore.

In spite of tossing and turning late into the night, in spite of the need to get up to do our last minute packing long before Gil and Harry arrived at 08:00, we didn't need an alarm clock. We were awake before dawn. By the time the first rays of light struck *Taleisin*'s snowy hull, we were sitting together on the hill above her building shed, trying to imagine what she'd look like with her eight-foot bowsprit in place, her 45-foot mast towering into the air. Larry was unnaturally quiet as he sat stroking the watch dog we'd grown a bit too fond of.

"What's wrong, Cindy?" he whispered to her. "Do you know we're abandoning you for *Seraffyn*?"

I looked at the two of them and then back at this brand new husky ship below us and for a fleeting second I too saw the ghost of the tiny ship that had previously shaped our years together.

During the three-hour trip down the tree-lined driveway, out the canyon road, twisting and turning and crossing the same trickling stream three times, along 50 miles of freeway and through the narrow streets of Old Newport Beach, *Seraffyn*'s ghost never once flitted across my mind. Even during the eight days we spent splicing wire, putting extra coats of varnish on the spars then finally lifting the mast into place, *Taleisin* was the one and only, the focus of our days, her personality entirely her own, from the seemingly huge 10'9" beam to her luxurious cushion-lined forward lounge and double bunk, from the strangeness of her flush-decked cockpit area to her gently curving deck boxes extending so naturally to her long, sleek cabin sides.

That ghost might have hidden from us because of our slightly more mature attitude towards *Taleisin*. We'd never been able to joke about *Seraffyn*. Every inch of her 24'4" length seemed too important to take for granted. But the sheer increase in size, an increase that seemed to be far more than you'd expect from having only 5'6" more length, or maybe the fact that we now knew we could build another boat and set off cruising another time let us feel far more relaxed about *Taleisin*. Encouraged by friends and family who began arriving a week before the scheduled party, we decorated the boat for her Halloween weekend launching. Bushy black, grease-penciled eyebrows graced the portlights on her bow. A hollowed out, 20-pound pumpkin grinned above the growing crowd, its nose the tip of *Taleisin*'s bowsprit. Windsocks flew from the spreaders to augment the traditional signal flag bunting strung along her forestay. Bunches of fresh flowers competed for attention with the fresh varnish of the cabin top hatches as almost 400 friends, family and well-wishers came pouring into Lido Shipyard carrying casseroles, salads, pastries and an enormous platter of fresh shrimp brought in that morning by the local fishermen. A dozen yachts, adorned with signal flags, sailed up the harbor to raft up and join the party.

At exactly noon, my niece Michelle swung a bottle of champagne against the bobstay fitting at *Taleisin*'s forefoot. Seconds after it exploded in a spray of foam, and *Taleisin*'s keel touched saltwater. Champagne corks exploded around me. Larry stood on deck looking like a proud Viking as she settled slowly into the water, then he leapt ashore to grab me and whisper, "When no one is looking, better take a look in her bilges – shouldn't take on much water but..." I found that chance only minutes later. A mere

Larry was born on Halloween. We've launched each of our boats on the same day. The pumpkin and eyebrows artfully drawn over Taleisin's *portlights were added by friends who clearly got into the spirit of the day.*

trickle meandered along the keel timber, just as I had expected. And in the momentary quiet of the cabin, memories of the hundreds of times I'd opened the floorboards on little *Seraffyn* to get out a bottle of wine or store away a jug of kerosene flashed through my mind. I could hear *Seraffyn* still whispering to me.

I shoved the ghost aside as I rushed back outside to join the celebration which carried on well past midnight.

Not only did Taleisin *get launched, but so did her two owner/builders. That is Lyle Hess, her designer, enjoying the moment as I waste some of the celebratory champagne.*

The ghost of *Seraffyn* kept her distance during the three weeks we spent getting *Taleisin* ready for her first foray under sail. As soon as daylight filled our cabin each morning, Larry was out on deck splicing the lower ends of the rigging wire, bolting fittings onto the boom, adding blocks to the taffrail. My mornings seemed to be filled with an almost daily bicycle journey round Newport Beach and Balboa to visit each of the five marine stores searching for just the right bolts, the right woodscrew to keep him satisfied. *Taleisin* was in such a constant state of upheaval that it was hard to decide what her decks would look like once all the sailing gear was in place.

Below decks the upheaval seemed more organized as I kept moving things from one place to another – but it was no easier to adjust and settle in. This boat had twice the storage space of *Seraffyn* but instead of making my life easier, the abundance of room added the confusion and frustration of decision making.

"Should I keep my baking goods in this end of the settee locker because that worked so well on *Seraffyn* or should I put them opposite the stove on the port side so I can get to them even if you are down below having lunch?" I asked Larry.

"Don't ask me," he answered. "Just don't take it so seriously. You aren't making irreversible decisions; you can always move things around later."

We both agreed to relegate the final interior refinements until we'd actually lived with the boat, gotten her out sailing and learned how we'd move around in her. The work list, taking up only two lined pages on my steno-sized pad, contained some time-consuming jobs for later: jobs like building a dinette table, creating bookshelves, adding lee clothes, towel racks, sea rails and even paper towel holders. We hoped that by waiting for experience to guide us, we'd design, build and install these amenities so they worked perfectly from the beginning. Besides, we were both thrilled to be afloat, delighted by the shore side sounds of squawking ducks and squabbling seagulls each morning and eager for that very first sail – the moment of truth when we'd know how this boat, which unlike *Seraffyn* had been designed just for us, felt as she stood to her first gusts of wind.

The day *Taleisin*'s boom was finally secured in place, her sails bent on and furled, a low pressure system moved onshore and collided with a ridge of high pressure over the inland deserts of southern California. Fifty-knot gusts howled as night fell. By morning rain blew through Balboa Bay and drove us into a local café to drink a half dozen cups of tea and coffee while we moaned about this latest delay. Two days later we both awake at dawn. The late November morning was crisp and clear. A light southerly wind promised to give us an easy first sail out of the restricted channel where *Taleisin* was moored. Since we had not yet rigged our sculling oar and since we had no bow anchor rollers installed, Larry rushed to set our 35-pound CQR anchor in the stern roller he'd built as part of our boomkin.[2] I already had our dock lines loosened and ready to go, the sails untied, the jumble of unfamiliar halyards sorted in my mind, when he called, "I'm ready – are you?"

Light zephyrs of wind barely ruffled the water as *Taleisin* glided, quietly as a ghost, down the quarter-mile-long channel. The morning was so still, we could hear alarm clocks going off in the homes on shore. The

2 A boomkin is a strong spar extending aft over the transom of a sailing yacht. The backstay is attached the outer end of the boomkin. Its purpose is to move the backstay far enough aft so the boom will clear the backstay during a gybe.

first joggers of the day waved from the walkway that circles Balboa Island while we drifted by on the incoming tide. Within minutes I was breathless. Partially it was the excitement of finally feeling *Taleisin* moving under her own power, but partially because I felt thoroughly rusty after spending so much time ashore, confused by winches mounted in places that were new to hands trained by thousands of hours on a different boat that looked so much like this one.

As soon as we were in clear water Larry climbed out onto the bowsprit, turned, then sat down facing aft to watch the stem part the water, to trace the lines of rigging for any possible foul-ups or need for potential improvements.

A few minutes later he called, "How about hauling in the sheets and beating up the bay?"

Seraffyn's ghost leapt mischievously on board. I reached for the mainsheet cleat and it wasn't there. I shoved the tiller with one hand to head her up and slid my other hand along the deck searching, my heart racing as I felt a momentary panic. Then I turned and remembered this wasn't *Seraffyn*. As much as the straight-laid teak deck and varnished bowsprit might remind me of her, this was a far different boat, one with an entirely different cockpit layout. I located the mainsheet cleat on the outer side of the deck box/seats that outlined the cockpit area and began hauling in the 75 feet of line that runs through seven blocks to form a six-part-purchase mainsheet. Meanwhile Larry had climbed back in from the bowsprit and was now working in unison with me, cranking in the sheet for our lapper, the 95 percent genoa we use as our working headsail. Then the first real gust of wind hit – wind we would have been expecting if our sailing skills weren't so rusty from disuse. The telltale signs had been there floating across the sky since we'd left the dock. Instead of having just eight or ten knots of wind for our maiden sailing tests, we now had 25.

"Better get ready to drop the jib," I called as that first strong gust hit.

For a moment I felt almost as if the spirits of the two boats were struggling for supremacy, and *Taleisin/Seraffyn* bucked and strained as we all gained our bearings. Then *Taleisin* seemed to exert her will. Instead of heeling until her waterways ran with foam, instead of demanding shorter sail by pulling on her rudder until I had to brace my feet against the far cockpit coaming just to keep control of the tiller, *Taleisin* surged forward and gracefully heeled just until her full-length rub rail touched the water. As she accelerated, her tiller hummed in my hand yet never seemed to increase its pull.

I felt my feet relax and I almost screamed, "She's stiff, she's stiff as hell!"

Six thousand six hundred pounds of lead under a boat that weighed just over 15,000 pounds, plus her wide-beamed, wineglass-shaped hull, let her pack canvas well beyond the limits of the boat she was replacing. And the speed: we crossed the familiar bay in half the time we remembered from our last days of sailing before we'd said farewell to *Seraffyn*.

"How does she feel?" Larry asked as he sat waiting for me to willingly relinquish the tiller.

"Wonderful, I think," was all I could say as I watched the fingers of white foam heralding the next gust and waited for the wind to reach us and test my newest love affair. "If she's this stiff now, what will she be like when we load another ton-and-a-half of gear and stores on board and get her down to her full displacement lines?"

Larry couldn't restrain himself any longer. "Come on, let's tack. You sheet in the jib this time. Let me feel her."

I reluctantly gave him the tiller and *Seraffyn*'s ghost tried to sneak on board once again.

"Ready about," Larry called. I let the starboard jib sheet fly and instinctively put my hand behind me to reach for the port sheet. It wasn't there. I turned to search the corner of the cockpit where that sheet had lain, ready at hand, day or night all across the years and oceans of sailing we'd shared. Now the brand new lapper was out of control, flogging wildly in the gusty wind.

"I hate this damned cockpit arrangement!" I cried as I searched outside the cockpit coaming seats and finally located the end of the leeward sheet.

"Come on, Lin, you haven't even given it a chance," Larry said as he pulled the tiller to ease the pressure on the jib while I finished winching in the sail. "What do you expect on your very first tack?" he added as he scrambled to brace himself in this new and unfamiliar cockpit.

I was glad it was a winter Monday and we were the only boat out on the water so early in the day. One out of every two tacks looked and felt sloppy as we beat up the long narrow northern leg of Newport Bay. But just as Larry predicted, each tack became a bit easier, the cockpit began to feel more logical as my feet found their brace points, and my knees learned where to rest.

After 20 minutes we eased the sheets and ran before the wind just to take a rest. Then we decided to anchor in the open area of the main turning basin while we ate lunch. With no other boats in the anchorage, we had lots of room to drift while we tried out the stern anchor roller for the first time. As soon as the boat settled down, her stern facing the wind,

Larry put the drop boards in place to block the cold wind and keep the flames on our propane stove from blowing out. Then we sat down to a warm lunch, a pad of note paper at hand for the inevitable additions we'd add to our work list.

The very first note read: *move bow roller installation to top priority.*

That first day of sailing trials taught us a lot about the boat we'd built. As much as she looked like her little sister *Seraffyn*, she amazed us with just how dissimilar she was. Some of the differences were easy to accept: her stiffness, her easy helm, her powerful winches and wider deck areas, her seemingly generous interior. Other differences would test our sailing skills and my strength and agility. The extra three-and-a-half tons of weight, the longer overall length (*Taleisin* measures 42 feet from boomkin end to bowsprit end; *Seraffyn* measures 33 feet overall) meant we had to bail out on our first attempt to round up into the berth we'd rented – she just didn't turn as sharply. Her sails were not only bulkier and heavier to move around on deck, but their larger area made them harder to winch in. Her far wider foredeck area left me feeling a bit insecure as handholds seemed just beyond my grasp.

As dusk began fading to dark, we secured *Taleisin*'s mooring lines then worked in quiet companionship furling her sails, coiling lines and then adding the newly arrived sail covers.

For the next two weeks we worked to install her ground tackle, tune her rig to our liking and secure the additional cleats we'd discovered we needed. Then we began adding the gear that we knew made sailing a relatively heavy vessel like this one easier for two people who prefer to handle night watches completely on their own: lazy jacks to control the mainsail as it is lowered into place atop the boom, a jib downhaul and lines to control the instant spinnaker pole arrangement.[3]

As we incorporated ideas we'd gained during our eleven years of cruising on *Seraffyn*, this new home began to take on a distinctive personality. Fittings we'd put up with on the littler boat because they were all we could get at the time didn't exist on *Taleisin*. Now we had exactly what we wanted because Larry had learned to make relatively sophisticated foundry patterns to cast the item he wanted, and then machine it for a perfect fit.

3 These are described in detail in *The Self-Sufficient Sailor.*

Gear we'd developed for *Seraffyn* through trial and error[4] worked right the first time as we re-created it to fit *Taleisin*.

Long before *Taleisin* was ready to go out into the open ocean for real sea-trials, we grew tired of just working. To keep our sanity, to whet our appetites anew and to check that the gear we were adding worked as we hoped it would, we set out on what we called a mini-cruise one sunny February morning. We cleaned the boat up inside and out, vacuuming away wood shavings and saw dust and storing all the tools and gear we'd brought on board but hadn't yet installed, then spent a day sailing around the five-mile-long bay. We anchored in the turning basin that night, then did some light-hearted racing against other friends we'd invited to meet up with us the next day.

Seraffyn's ghost receded as we set sail and headed out the bay. *Taleisin* was fast becoming our complete and only home as we savored her dedicated bathing amenities, her comparatively immense lockers, her soft, velvet-covered settees and her wide-open floor spaces. Each maneuver seemed much smoother as the flush-decked cockpit area began to feel familiar and my hands began to know where to reach to find each sheet, each halyard.

Time after time that day, we beat up the five-mile-long bay, then ran back down its length wing and wing on a steady southwesterly breeze, only to turn and once again beat back out towards the breakwater, which seemed to beckon with arms spread wide, as if urging us to keep on sailing towards the open horizon. But we weren't ready; nor was *Taleisin*. So each time we felt the heave of the ocean swell, we turned to head back into the protected waters of the bay.

Late in the afternoon, as the mid-winter sun was just setting, and the cold was beginning to creep beyond our exhilaration, we spotted two handsome voyaging boats lying at anchor in the turning basin. Thirty-one-foot *Sprinkle*, a fiberglass cutter from Seattle, had smoke simmering from its stack. As we lowered our sails and, for the first time ever, eased *Taleisin*'s bow anchor out using the brand new windlass, I noticed puffs of smoke coming from the stack on 27-foot *Clara*, a gaff-rigged wooden sloop hailing from Tacoma. The rattle of our chain brought her owners, Bruce and Carrie Dobbin, out on deck to wave a friendly hello. By the time the cold, cutting wind had lain down and the crisp winter stars filled the sky, all three couples were ensconced in *Sprinkle*'s main saloon, becoming acquainted over aromatic cups of tea and fresh lemon cake. The names of

4 One example of this is the windvane self-steering. People ask us who designed it. Larry's answer: "It wasn't designed; it evolved. Designs work right the first time."

mutual cruising friends popped into the conversation. Sailing tales from Alaska, stories of ports we'd all visited in the Puget Sound, discussions of the voyaging and ports waiting for us south of the border hurried the night along.

And then, as we rowed home, smiling from the evening's stories and warmed by the promise it offered – a prelude to the life we were rejoining – that's when I saw *Seraffyn* again, sitting there, waiting.

Or rather, *Seraffyn*'s ghost.

I realized her ghost would never disappear completely. We would see it less frequently as we went on to explore places *Seraffyn* had never taken us, as we weathered storms in a cabin warmed by the vented heater *Seraffyn* never had. But I came to feel her ghost as a special gift, a reminder that size never mattered, that sea-worthiness alone outweighed all other traits. *Seraffyn*'s ghost lingered as a reminder that the ultimate luxury is time granted to do what we enjoyed most. All the comforts *Taleisin* could provide would mean nothing unless she was used to gain us the freedom and adventures *Seraffyn* had provided so well.

Bob Grieser took this shot of Taleisin *only a few weeks after we got her out sailing.*
The reefing genoa, which had worked well on Seraffyn, was not as successful on this larger boat.
In New Zealand it was replaced with a bonneted genoa.
(See Cost Conscious Cruiser *for more details.)*

The first time we actually saw our own boat under sail.
Doug Schmuck headed out for a day of sailing on 28-foot BCC Puffin. *Once clear of the breakwaters we left a friend in charge of* Taleisin *and climbed onto* Puffin.

CHAPTER 2

ALMOST CRUISING

"We're cruising."

Larry smiled. "We're doing sea trials."

Looking back at those eight months we spent sailing the waters of Southern California, never venturing further than 120 miles from where we'd launched *Taleisin*, I still find it hard to decide which of us was closest to the truth.

On New Year's Eve, two months after *Taleisin* touched the water, with the rigging sorted, reefing gear in place and ground tackle fully installed, we set sail from Newport Beach for our first foray onto open waters. Our goal, Catalina Island, lay just 31 miles to the west.

Southern California is known for its light winds, normally ranging from five to fifteen knots. But a Santa Ana wind had been predicted for late that night. This is a relatively rare occurrence during the mid-winter months. Usually Santa Anas occur in autumn when the colder, heavier air of the high desert flows downward through the steep canyons of the coastal mountains, gathering speed as it drops thousands of feet to meet

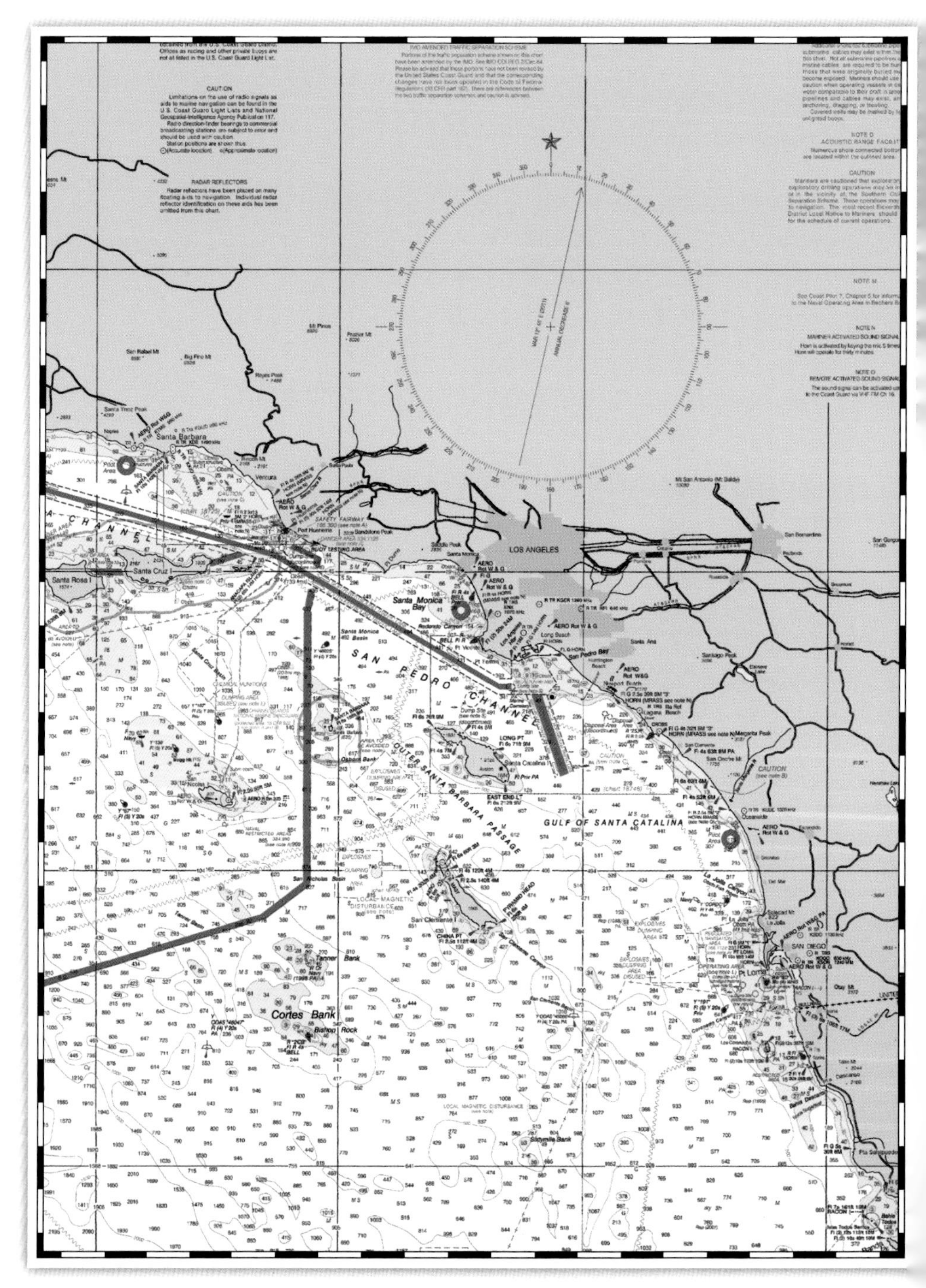

We roamed as far south as San Diego, then north and west along the coast of Southern California to Santa Barbara and the Channel Islands during our sea trials.

the warmer waters of the Pacific. Though we were slightly skeptical about the forecast, we shaped a course towards Cat Harbor, a fully enclosed bay on the western side of the 22-mile-long island, rather than heading towards an anchorage on the eastern side of the island which is normally protected from the prevailing northwesterly winds.

The first warm, dry gust came roaring across the open waters just before dark. The Santa Ana caught us eight miles from Cat Harbor. That 40-knot blast proved *Taleisin* was still a fair-weather boat. Though the jib downhaul and reefing pennants were usable, Larry's frustration as he rushed to shorten sail showed they needed some more adjusting. I felt clumsy and uncomfortable with no lifelines to grab hold of as I went forward to help tie the third reef into the mainsail. With no boom-gallows to lean against as I took bearings on the lighthouse on Santa Barbara Island, twelve miles further west, I felt vulnerable and had a hard time steadying my hand-bearing compass to read the numbers. The dinghy, secured to hastily thrown-together temporary brackets on the cabin top, threatened to come loose as the boat lunged through the growing seas. Gear inside the boat tumbled from lockers that needed stronger latches to secure their contents.

Darkness fell as we neared the northwestern tip of Catalina. But the guiding beams of lighthouses on three different islands could be seen clearly in the crisp dry air and absolutely clear skies created by the Santa Ana. Both of us were relieved to reach the calm waters in the lee of the island, even though the steep high cliffs turned our blasting romp into a quiet drift as we drew closer to the small protected bay. There was only a zephyr of wind as we short-tacked between the protecting arms of Cat Harbor and wove our way past the handful of boats that lay at anchor. Just as Larry went forward to let go the main halyard, I heard the ship's clock on the nearest yacht begin to chime – midnight. Then came the slightly more distant chime from a motorboat anchored further up the bay, which was joined by the rich ringing of our beautiful new ship's bell.

Eight bells, and 1984 became a reality.

Larry was on deck soon after daybreak, coffee cup in hand, surveying his kingdom and watching a bright red *San Juan* 24 sloop as it beat up the bay. At the helm, a lightly-built young woman stood clad in salt-stained foul weather gear. Tangled and twisted blond hair showed she'd felt the might of the Santa Ana wind too.

"You on your own?" Larry called over.

Gracie Sims, standing proud though weather-beaten, yelled, "Just completing my qualifying voyage for the solo Trans-Pacific race."

Larry leaned his head inside the cabin and we had a quick whispered conference before he called back, "Soon as you anchor, come on over and have a hot shower and hot coffee too."

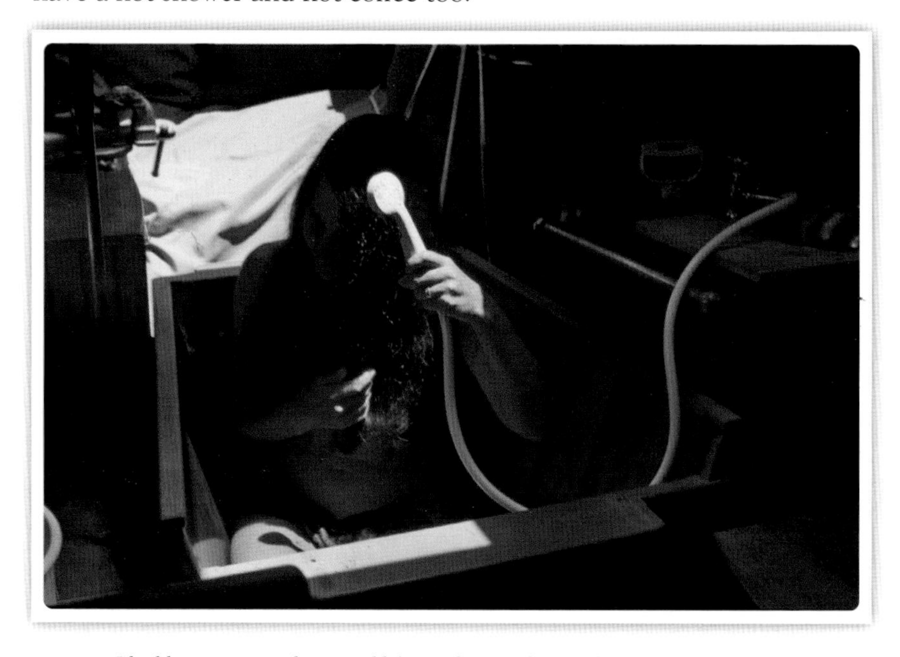

I had been concerned we wouldn't use the sitztub enough to justify the space it took. Within a few weeks afloat my doubts vanished, especially as its position let us safely shower even when we were offshore during heavy weather.

Soon afterwards Larry set off in the dinghy to take a look at some of the other boats anchored near us. Meanwhile, I escorted this grateful singlehanded racing sailor into our cabin, warmed to a cozy 75 degrees by our newly installed kerosene heating stove, and demonstrated how to use the hand-pumped hot water system. As I brewed up a fresh pot of coffee I felt downright smug thinking about all the times we'd gratefully accepted shower invitations from folks on bigger boats when winter made on-deck showering totally uninviting. Now, we had our own warm shower to offer and enjoy ourselves: the shower/sitztub Larry had fashioned to fit just below the companionway where most other boats have engines.

"That felt great," Gracie commented as she toweled off and began pulling on fresh, clean clothes. "Not many folks who would give up this much space just for a shower."

"Larry's definitely sexier when he's clean," I jokingly told Gracie. Which is true, but, even more than that, I was glad Larry had insisted on this innovation as now we could cruise through colder seasons and higher latitudes much more enjoyable – and even be the ones doing the occasional inviting!

As we waited for the Santa Ana winds to abate, we seemed to spend an inordinate amount of time with our work list open, adding new jobs, prioritizing jobs, classifying jobs into woodworking, metal working, rigging and sail-making categories.

"If we do all of the same kind of jobs at the same time we shouldn't have so many tools spread around," I stated as I put the list in order.

Larry nodded then said, "I think that's the lot. Now if we work efficiently, we should be able to get this all done in a month, maybe less. This job should only take an hour. That one should only take a few minutes."

But when we returned to our rented slip in Newport Beach, the list, and the time each job took, seemed to magically expand. For three and a half months we worked towards making *Taleisin* into an all-weather, blue-water voyager and wrote articles to fatten our cruising kitty – all the while setting aside time to share with the friends and family we'd be leaving behind.

Life on board was often chaotic. Our chores often seemed to collide. Even with an early morning planning session we didn't seem able to synchronize our projects. Larry pulled the floor boards out to fit brass stanchions for our inclining saloon table just when I wanted to cut plastic mesh liners to protect the inside of the settee storage lockers; similarly, I wanted to put provisions into the forward cabin just as Larry chose that moment to add new locks to every cabinet in the boat. On deck, fresh varnish and paint work lived under the constant threat of sawdust as Larry drilled and sawed, planed and sanded at the portable work bench he'd clamped to the dock beside *Taleisin*.

But by mutual agreement, a work truce was called every two weeks. We cleaned up our tools, put *Taleisin* back in order, then spent two or three days reminding ourselves what we were fighting for, re-whetting our appetite by using our private magic carpet. We'd sail twelve miles south to anchor at Dana Point, or fifteen miles north to meander the waterways of Long Beach/Los Angeles Harbor. Some days we'd take friends along; others we'd go alone. Each time we sailed, we composed yet another work list.

By mid-April *Taleisin* was truly a home and felt like a seaworthy offshore boat, but she still wasn't a tried-and-true blue-water cruiser. For one thing, we needed to ensure we had a reliable windvane. We'd built a prototype windvane out of cedar, Delrin, plywood and Dacron that seemed to work well for day sailing. But we both agreed it needed more testing in varied

Cheeky *was designed by Lyle Hess to fit on board* Taleisin. *The plug that Larry built was then purchased by the Fatty Knees boat company. Larry claims he named* Cheeky *after me. Here we are anchored in Long Beach, near the Queen Mary.*

conditions before we felt comfortable finalizing the design and building it from more durable materials. We also needed to add locks to each of the floor boards. But we were very close. Our sails now set to perfection; the rigging was detailed to exactly the state that made me smile each time I glanced at the carefully turned cotter pins, the smoothly seized jib net, and the chafe-preventing covers on each shroud where the mainsail might rub. *Taleisin*'s shining newness had taken on a more sedate patina.

But our cruising plans were now hampered by the seasons. We dreamed of renewing our memories of Mexico's Baja California and the warm waters of the Gulf of California before setting off across an ocean, but from June to October hurricanes made these waters too insecure to be inviting, especially for an untried boat.

Then an invitation arrived that solved our dilemma.

The San Diego Maritime Museum was hosting the launch of a replica revenue cutter, *Californian*.[1] We were invited to be one of the picket boats, anchored right at the front line to mark out the restricted area. In the same packet of mail there was another invitation. This one asked if we would like to join the Old Timers Regatta for wooden boats at the same port but one week later.

"Let's do it," Larry said. "We can meander down to San Diego, and then beat back north until we find some real wind to test the boat. It's been eighteen years since I've been to the Channel Islands. We've never really been tourists in places like Ventura or Santa Barbara. Maybe we can find some other races we can join."

So in early May, we loaded most of Larry's tools into their on-board storage lockers for the very first time, folded our two bicycles into their padded carry bags and slid them into the lazarette. Then we took on stores to last at least four weeks and consigned our trusty old GMC pick-up truck to a friend's care. Free of all other shore-side possessions, we set sail and encountered the type of adventures we usually associated with foreign shores.

We'd often driven down to San Diego to shop for timber and boatbuilding supplies. Before we'd parted with *Seraffyn*, we'd even taken a sailing holiday and spent a week as guests of the San Diego yacht club. But, with a shiny

1 *Californian* is actually a topsail schooner and a very close replica of the 1847 Revenue Cutter, CW *Lawrence*.

new boat to play with, no real schedule and *Californian*'s launching party to kick-start our stay, we set out to explore a San Diego that would now present a completely different face to us.

Moments after we arrived we learned that being a water-born visitor in San Diego can be problematic: the bay is crowded with yachts, local fish boats, naval vessels, submarines, plus occasional seaplanes. Yacht clubs, shipyards and moorings seem to fill most of the shoreline and, though we spotted dozens of potential places that looked like they'd offer shelter, we learned that anchoring was limited to a few days each in six different carefully designated places. Meanwhile, harbor officials were, for want of a better word, officious – if you happened to drop anchor for even a few minutes anywhere else.

Fortunately the harbor patrol eased its restrictions for the planned 1900 hour launching of *Californian* at Spanish Bay.[2] Soon after noon we sailed close to the site where flags were being strung to decorate the handsome lines of the racy-looking, historically accurate ship. A rowing skiff set off from shore to meet us and indicate where we were to anchor. Over the next hours we saw why we and two other distinctive yachts had been asked to serve as "Picket Boats." By launching time the narrow waterway was jammed with a fleet of more than 300 vessels, ranging from kayaks to 150-foot tugs. On shore, 5000 people cheered as the crashing sound of the traditional champagne bottle was carried out across the water by loud speakers. Slowly the huge trailer under *Californian* began to creep towards the water, the cheering turned to one *Oh no!* after another. *Californian* began to lean. The trailer stopped, mired in the mud of the shoreline. The collective gasp of the onlookers was audible for miles. But, the celebrations continued as if nothing had happened. Bands played just 50 feet from where *Californian* sat on her mired launching trailer, leaning ten degrees to port. Fireworks lit the evening sky above her. The party carried on till midnight and we were informed by the harbor patrol that we should stay at anchor as we would be needed for the second launch attempt the next day.

A dozen visitors floated by the next day: old friends who'd been out to watch *Taleisin* being built, other folks we'd just met. We had a ringside view of the shore-side activities as two huge cranes worked to lift *Californian* and her cradle clear of the mud, and then shift her to a firm bit of shoreline. As the evening's high tide approached, only a dozen boats were in attendance. *Californian* slid smoothly into the water and we

2 At the time of this launching party there were neither marinas nor hotels at Spanish Landing. But anchoring was not allowed due to Spanish Landing's use by the naval academy for training purposes.

rowed in to join her building crew for a celebration much more intimate than the one we'd been party to the day before.

Just after midnight we rowed back to *Taleisin* and climbed into our warm sleeping bags. Unfortunately we soon learned the harbor patrol's forbearance had ended.

"This is a restricted area. Move immediately," demanded the same skipper who had earlier lay alongside to enjoy the festivities.

"There's no wind; we've got no engine. Can't we wait until the breeze springs up in the morning?" Larry asked.

"No!" he stated. "Just got a call from the higher-ups. You've got to move right now."

And so, our late-night sail back to the visitor's anchorage at La Playa started out grudgingly.

Soon however, Larry turned the tide. "There's just a tickle of a breeze – feel it?" he said. "Let's look at this as one more part of our sea trials. Good chance to try out the hanks we've added to the nylon drifter."

As the crowds gathered to watch the launching of Californian, *we felt privileged to act as one of the boats marking the limit of the anchorage. This gave us front row seats for the event.*

As soon as the anchor was cranked in and secured, Larry set to work pulling the 1.5-ounce blue, green and white nylon sail out of its bag. I helped lead the sheet to the end of the boom. Then Larry hoisted the high cut, genoa-sized sail and it caught the breeze. But its outline against the star-filled sky looked strange. Larry cleated the halyard then turned on his flashlight to check the sail.

"Well, that's another item for the work list," he commented. "Guess we're going to have to add some markings so we can tell the tack from the head of the drifter if we want to fly it right-side up."

Many years ago, while we were exploring the shores of the Mediterranean Sea, we'd written a list of the most important space-consuming items we'd add if ever we built a larger boat to replace 24'4" *Seraffyn*. The list was surprisingly short: an easy-to-use indoor shower, a heater, a designated workbench/tool storage area and a storage spot below decks for folding bicycles.

It was great to be afloat. Now we had time to share with friends since the hard work of building was behind us. This is part of a page from Taleisin's *first logbook.*

Within a few days of moving on board *Taleisin* one or the other of us would invariably ask, "Okay, what's today's 'best idea we ever had'?"

All during our stay in San Diego the folding bicycles topped the list.

Gone was my resentment of the large amount of space we'd had to set aside in *Taleisin*'s lazarette, the expense of creating special oil-resistant padded bags to protect both the varnish work of the boat's interior and the bikes themselves. From the moment we lifted the bicycles, with their 22" wheels, nylon saddle bags and panniers fore and aft, onto the dock at Shelter Island, we loved this new addition to our cruising life. They turned grocery shopping and laundry into a game. By carefully balancing our load, we found we could carry a week's worth of groceries between us, plus two 50-pound blocks of ice and a gallon box of wine, all in one trip. Armed with a visitor's guide, a picnic lunch, straw sunhats and a small beach blanket, we pedaled through the parks we'd never before taken time to visit, stopped to admire museums and art installations, ate ice cream cones on the beach then returned to the boat late in the day without the sore feet or stressed budget that had, in times past, curtailed our desire to act like tourists.

The *Old Timers Regatta* proved once again that the way to really learn about your boat – the way to improve your sailing skills quickly – is to pit yourself against other sailors by joining into occasional organized races. For *Taleisin*'s first serious race, we had gathered an enthusiastic crew, willing, eager and with some knowledge of the local waters and weather patterns. The wind was fresh, growing from twelve knots to eighteen, with occasional gusts to 22 knots. We were delighted with *Taleisin*'s speed as she kept up with 35- to 38-footers. Our crew was impressed and could hardly believe our performance – until we reminded them *Taleisin*'s plumb stem and almost vertical stern gave her a waterline that was almost the same as the longer modern boats.

As we'd expected, the race added a few items to our work list. The most expensive and time-consuming: build new spinnaker pole. The 20-foot pole Larry shaped from a 3-by-3-inch piece of spruce had been serving us well until now. But in the fresh winds of the race it scared us all by bending almost three feet when we tried reaching with our three-quarter-sized spinnaker. Then there was the jumble of lines that turned the cockpit into a spaghetti pit when the boom vang and pole downhaul were added to spinnaker sheet, spinnaker guy plus both ends of our double-ended mainsheet. That added items number 27 through 29 to the work list: move mainsheet cleats outside the cockpit, add cleat for boom vang, install cleat for downhaul line. It took us almost a year to cross the last two items off the list. In order to keep the lines clear of the cockpit but within easy reach of the helm, we eventually mounted a pair of bronze cam-cleats on the aft corners of the cabin top.

Following the regatta, we spent almost a week in Mariners Basin, in Mission Bay, only twelve miles north of San Diego. This peaceful place reminded Larry and me of Balboa Island as we'd known it when we first met, 20 years before. The quiet cove, situated just off the main channel, is protected from all winds and has excellent holding ground and lovely beaches. An assortment of novice surf sailors added constant amusement to each day as their spectacular flops and gradual successes brought them whizzing past our boat. Jim and Marty Carnevale, two sailors we'd met in San Diego, arrived three days later to anchor their 40-footer not far from us. We put our work list aside and forgot about sea trials to share two days of quiet friendship; the intense, get-to-know-each-other, spend-all-day-talking kind of companionship usually found only when you are really out cruising and unhampered by shore-side pressures or telephones.

Then, a few days later, the outside world came back into our life. We'd made a date to join another race in Long Beach. At dawn, Larry began to crank in our anchor chain. *Clink, clank, clink, clank, clink, clank, clank… thunk, thud, thud.* The familiar sound of gears and palls moving inside a bath of heavy oil suddenly changed. I heard the sound of a spring snapping. The chain stopped feeding into the locker. *Taleisin* is outfitted with 300 feet of 5⁄16" hi-test chain plus an assortment of anchors ranging in weight from 22 pounds to 65 pounds. Ron Amy, a boat builder-turned-cruiser we'd met on board his 35-foot sloop in the Philippines, had returned from several years afloat and set to work building hardware for cruising boats. He and Larry had come up with a prototype bronze two-speed hand-operated anchor windlass. It fit perfectly on top of the inboard end of our bowsprit where it could feed chain down through the hawse pipe and into our chain locker. My job was to go below decks and climb across the forward bunk, then settle comfortably against the cushions from where I could reach into the chain locker to flake the incoming chain. If we didn't do this, it formed a steep pile that could, in rough conditions, fall over on itself and cause the chain to jam next time we needed it.

That is why I'd heard the spring snap, and now that the chain had stopped feeding in, I rushed on deck then stood by helplessly as Larry pulled the anchor in hand over hand.

Between curses and grunts, he reminded me again, "That's why we're on sea trials."

The day after the Long Beach race, the windlass was shipped off and for the next two weeks we sailed without it while Ron and his crew dug around inside the sealed bronze casing and found the weak link. It was during this time that we both began to realize the importance of that bulky, heavy piece of cruising gear. Without it, I was not strong enough to retrieve our chain and anchor – something I'd been able to do on board *Seraffyn* with her smaller, lighter ground tackle. This meant I would be reluctant to sail the boat without Larry on board unless the windlass was 100 percent reliable. I needed the security of knowing, should Larry become ill or incapacitated, that I could take over and sail towards safety. Just as important, without that windlass there was the danger that either of us might strain or injure our back each time we handled the ground tackle.

So we learned new lessons and re-learned old ones as we cruised and explored, raced and played along the sun-drenched southern California coastline. In Long Beach we anchored only a few hundred yards from the towering bow of the *Queen Mary*, put on our fanciest clothes and rowed ashore for dinner and dancing surrounded by the art deco glamour of this romantic old ship. In Santa Barbara we explored the miles of bicycle paths where even pedestrians had to give way to our two-wheeled conveyances. We strolled past open air art shows, ate delicious hot tacos under the trees that line the wide sandy beaches. Better yet we watched as a smart-looking steel ketch sailed in, recognizing it as the *Scaldis*. When she came alongside we were delighted to renew our friendship with Cole Weston, a sailor-photographer we hadn't seen since we'd shared an anchorage in Costa Rica fifteen years before.

When the Mark IV version of our anchor windlass arrived, complete with an explanation of the problem that had caused the previous model to fail, we set sail for a place that was the complete antithesis of mainland California. Santa Rosa Island is an isolated, rocky, desert-like island lying 30 miles south of Cape Conception. Here, in complete solitude, we stayed for five days while the wind gusted to 35 knots. We never launched our dinghy. We did little but read, talk, eat, relax. We tested our windlass and gradually gained faith in its ability to handle our heavy ground tackle. We came to feel the experimentation had been worthwhile when we found we could crank our chain in at about three times the speed of any other hand windlass we'd seen. We tried the vented kerosene heater, round-wicked and blue-flamed, that we'd converted to fit inside a wood-burning stove body – and found the flame was being blown out too easily by the gusty winds rushing down the hills surrounding our anchorage. We studied, by way of comparison, the vents on our external oil lamps, which we knew could withstand wind gusts of over 50 knots: they had a funnel-shaped vent above the flames. So we used bits of metal we had on board to recreate a similar funnel for inside the stove smoke head. And now that it would stay lit, the hassle of installing the stove was relegated to the back of our minds as we enjoyed the adjustable, even heat it provided – heat we appreciated even though it was mid-August.[3]

When we tired of our absolute laziness, the constant gusty wind, the cold and often foggy dampness and the solitude, we hoisted our anchor and ran to Santa Cruz Island where we shared the anchorage at Prisoners Harbor with fifteen other boats. And here, in true cruising fashion, one hello led to a shared feast of abalone and fresh fish, red wine and homemade bread, plus an invitation to sail onward to Channel Islands Harbor for a dock party and another regatta. Unfettered by schedules and with no distinct plans for the next month, we took up the invitation and soon found ourselves tied alongside a dock among a dozen liveaboards who were hoping to set off cruising in the near future.

Each morning we watched as our new friends rushed off to work. Each weekend they got up early to work on their boats. They stole an hour here, a few hours there to fuel their dreams by talking with us. Their industriousness – the strict structure of their lives – not only reminded us of our good fortunate but made Larry and me face one of the new challenges in our own life: income.

From the time we first set off voyaging on *Seraffyn*, almost 20 years before, we'd had no set income. We had set aside sufficient savings in a secure place to cover six months of living. Then we we'd worked for three or four months each year until we had enough to cruise for another eight or nine months. We'd deliver boats for people with more money than time, or Larry would take on rigging jobs or boat repair work at shipyards along the way and I would work as his apprentice and finisher. We'd used this work time, usually three to four months each year, to refit *Seraffyn*, and as soon as the kitty and the boat were in good condition we set off exploring again. Only when our kitty began to grow low would we start sailing towards a port where we surmised there might be work for us. After four years of voyaging I'd started writing stories for magazines. Though I often scribbled notes on night watches and sometimes filled rainy days

3 Interestingly, we happened to be sitting on board *Taleisin* a few months ago, almost 35 years after setting sail from California, when Larry said to me, "Everything on this boat has been completely satisfying and worth the effort it took to get it working – except maybe that stove. I'd only give it a 50 percent success rating." I agree with him. In retrospect, a less attractive but well proven commercial kerosene heater such as that made by the German company Eberspacher probably would have been a better choice.

typing away at an article idea, I usually did the bulk of my writing while Larry was working ashore. When Larry decided to try writing too, he'd done it during our work periods, taking a day each week away from being a shipwright. We'd send the articles we produced to various editors hoping they would buy them. Then we'd sail off again. When checks arrived at unexpected intervals, they were like a special bonus. They were not something we counted on to determine the financial viability of our voyaging. And then, during the time we spent building *Taleisin*, I had achieved my goal of supporting the project by being a "real writer," working at a desk every day to create not only a stream of articles but four books. This led to something I think every writer craves: the offer of a guaranteed monthly fee to write exclusively for one magazine. It seemed a dream situation. The editors at *SAIL* magazine made it clear Larry and I could choose the topics we'd write about. In return, they wanted a guarantee of ten stories each year.

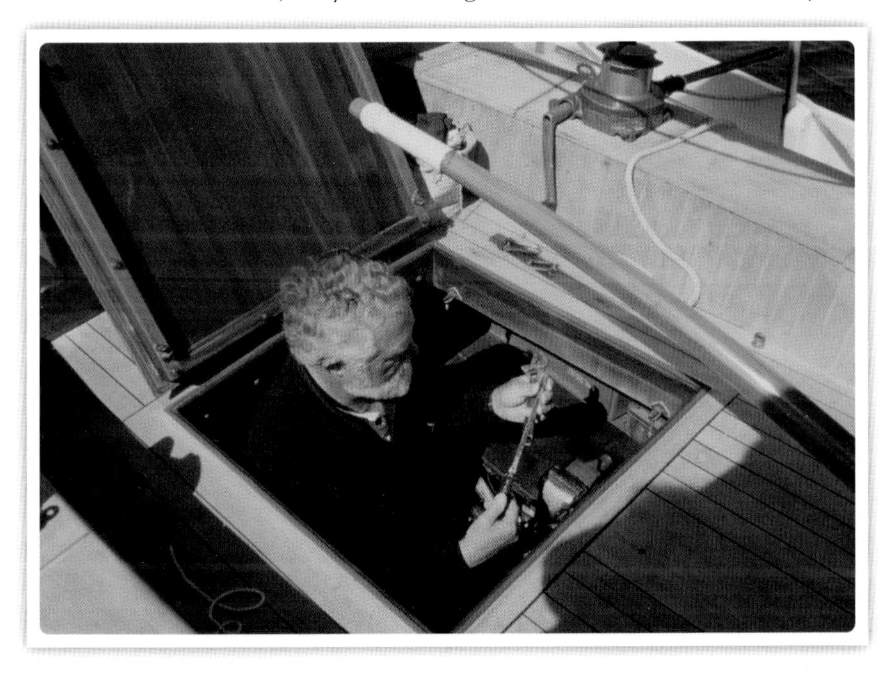

Larry jokingly says, "The workshop has full standing headroom." Then he adds, "If you open the cockpit hatch."

"No problem," I'd said. I'd easily written that many when we'd cruised on *Seraffyn*. I'd been writing far more than that as I lived in Bull Canyon helping to build *Taleisin*. Now we were back afloat, I wouldn't have the distraction of boatbuilding and home making, and with this new contract we wouldn't have to search for work each year to top up our cruising kitty.

Now we felt we would have lots of time to write.

But so far it didn't seem to be happening. In fact, the writing seemed an intrusion in our life afloat instead of a pleasant addition.

"Discipline," Larry said a day or two after we tied up in Channel Islands. "That's what writing takes and up until now we haven't been in the mood to be disciplined. So don't beat yourself up. But why don't we stay right here for two or three weeks and spend every morning writing? If we get two or three stories finished you can relax."

As we voyaged onward, this same scenario was played out almost three times a year: we'd fall behind on our writing obligations, become wracked with guilt, then find some place to stop for three or four weeks and make writing an almost full-time occupation. Eventually these writing breaks became a welcome part of our voyaging, a reason to stop moving, to find a safe anchorage and settle down until our work was finished, a virtual holiday from a life that to people ashore must seem like a constant holiday.

And so we settled into a comfortable rhythm in a marina berth fronting the Channel Islands Yacht Harbor. The long summer evenings and the light breezes that wafted across the protected waters of Channel Islands' large man-made water-ways were perfect for sailing our tender, *Cheeky*. Larry set up her rig within two days of our arrival. Her bright orange and yellow sail seemed to attract every other sailing dinghy in the harbor. Soon *Taleisin* had become the informal committee boat for what came to be known as the "Evening Apple and Oranges Regatta." Before the week was out rules had been created, a giant lollipop became the hotly contested grand prize and we all agreed to exchange dinghies for each subsequent race and score not the boat, but the skipper. This gave more people a chance to sail over the 20-minute course and showed that the performance of even the slowest appearing dinghy could be improved by a clever skipper. Not only did we enjoy the camaraderie this created but each of us got a chance to know *Cheeky* better and as we did, yet another half dozen to-do items were added to the ever-present work list, including two rows of reefs for her single sail.

Taleisin's racing career was most gratifying that summer. In response to the launching of *Californian*, several wooden boat clubs got together and set up a series of races all along the Southern Californian coast. They convinced seven different clubs to offer two weeks' free mooring for classic boats. Almost two dozen boat crews took up the offer and would race on one weekend, joined by dozens of local boats, both wooden and otherwise. Then the next weekend they'd cruise north to leave their boat in position, ready for the subsequent weekend of racing. This was particularly good for us as we could measure the effects of our upgrades and refits by judging *Taleisin*'s speed and handiness against other boats we knew. And, as we came to know our gear – as we adjusted and re-adjusted our rig, found better sheet leads, as well as better sheeting angles, and moved weight around inside the boat – we watched our speed increase until we beat boats that had passed us when *Taleisin* was brand new. Those nine races were a wonderful and intensive training ground for us. They encouraged us to carry canvas longer than we would have if we were only cruising, to put up more sail when we became confident of our rigging; they made us more willing to push the boat and ourselves. We also learned we needed a winch to assist us with our mainsail reefing outhaul pennant, an extra set of cam cleats for the spinnaker pole downhaul and extra page for the work list.

There was an added bonus to this harbor hopping regatta: my folks, who lived exactly in the middle of the itinerary's geography, suggested they come south to San Diego to watch us race and join in the after-race festivities when we first told them about our summer plans. Mom couldn't be just a by-stander. Instead she showed up early on the day of the first race, carrying all the fixings for a buffet breakfast for our crew of five. She had

We hauled Taleisin *out of the water before we departed for Mexico to install the finalized windvane. At the same time Larry chiseled off the seam putty which had squeezed out due to the expected swelling of the teak planking.*

great nibbles waiting when we came back in late in the day – windblown and full of tales of clever tacks, missed opportunities. By the third regatta a half dozen other crews had begun recruiting "support teams." But none seemed to surpass Mom who swept any unsupported team under her wing. The only down side of this support was the reminder that farewells were going to be much harder when the end of the Mexican hurricane season heralded our imminent departure.

When we sailed back into Newport Harbor for the last time in mid-September to take on stores and charts, we still had a page-long list of things to do before we set sail for Mexico in October. But that list was down mainly to small items such as adding chaffing gear on the bowsprit where the anchor shackle sometimes hit, holders for the 70-year-old crystal hanging flower vases my mother had given us, a galley strap for the cook.

The biggest work item of all was to build the final metal version of the windvane self-steering gear we'd been testing all summer. But now, after 800 miles of sailing in winds from almost calm to 45 knots, from hard beats to soft, smooth reaches, we felt good about investing the time and money this final piece of gear would require.

For two weeks as we worked through the last items on our work list, we discussed those months I'd called cruising and Larry had called sea trials. They'd really been both, and more besides. By exploring close to home we'd been able to test our gear and, if necessary, send it back to the manufactures relatively easily. By having all of the boat equipment on board before we left the country, we became familiar with it and devised ways to make sailing *Taleisin* easier while we could still find the specialized little bits and pieces we needed for each improvement. Because we didn't have the added complication of being in a foreign country with a foreign language, the small problems associated with getting to know a new sailing machine seemed less frustrating. By the end of that summer, there was no doubt in our minds: *Taleisin* had been transformed into a blue-water voyaging boat – more fun to sail, easier to handle, faster. Best of all, we'd made new friends and had fine adventures along the coastline we'd thought of as home.

As we set sail for Mexico and points south and west, we took with us the memories of a California we'd never known before.

We learned the hard way to avoid white nylon for our drifter and spinnaker. The white fabric rotted within two years of tropical sailing while the colored panels still had most of their strength.

With her 10'9" beam and 44 percent ballast to displacement ratio, Taleisin *proved to be much stiffer and more able to power to windward than* Seraffyn *had been. Mike Anderson took this photo when he and his partner Lauren joined us for a week of Baja California cruising.*

Chapter 3

You Can Only Do Something for the First Time Once

"A full moon. Venus high and bright in the evening sky," I wrote in the logbook. "So much ambient light there is no need to turn on the compass light. A reaching breeze ruffles the seas just enough to give *Taleisin* a surging rhythm as her taffrail log registers a continuous 6.6 knots."

I'll never forget the night we left San Diego bound south for Mexico after eleven months of preparations and sea trials. Each moment seemed to be full of both possibilities and memories. I'd gone below into the spacious feeling main cabin and listened to Larry's even breathing as he slept in the pilot berth on our very first night watch of *Taleisin*'s very first ocean passage. I moved quietly through the cabin to get a cold drink from the galley, and tried not to wake Larry. But he stirred in his sleep, then woke.

"Remember what an adventure this had felt like on *Seraffyn*?" he said.

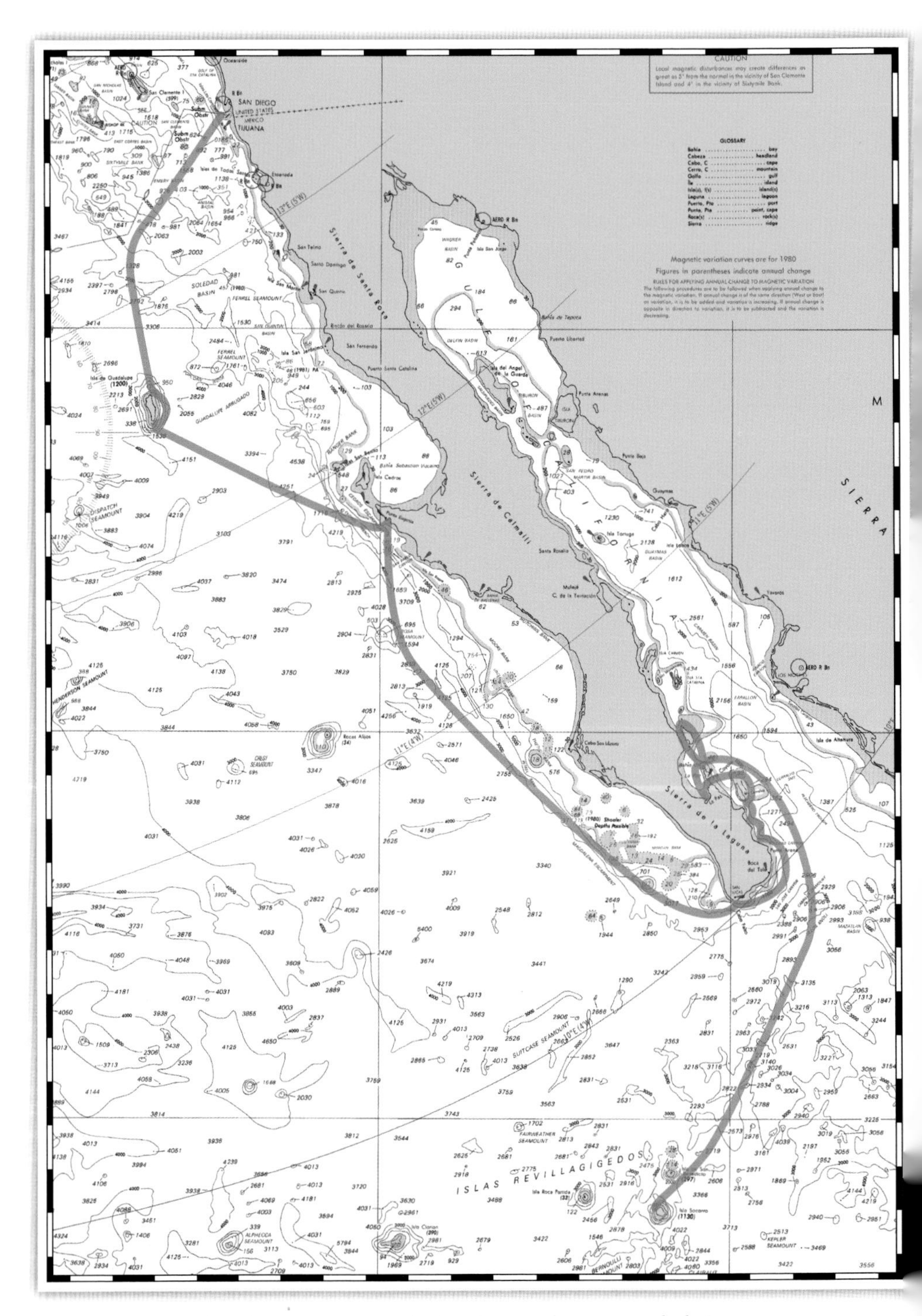

Our route from San Diego and into the Sea of Cortez then on toward Isla Socorro.

"I sure feel better prepared this time. We've got better gear, we're carrying far more provisions, our windvane works perfectly." As he turned to go back to sleep, he chuckled and added, "And so do you!"

I went out into the cockpit, scanned the horizon then settled on the sill of the companionway to watch for ships' lights as I recalled my almost cruise-shattering bout of seasickness fifteen years before when we'd left San Diego on board *Seraffyn*, bound for my first foreign landfall, the Mexican island of Guadalupe. I'd been downright scared back then, scared that I wouldn't like the adventure Larry had invited me to share, scared that I'd be unable to handle the chores of a sea-going life, scared that Larry would see through my bravado and laugh at my inner fears.

In spite of all my doubts, our cruising life had succeeded beyond my wildest imaginings. A voyage we hoped might last six months or a year continued on and on for eleven full, wonderful years until we crossed our outward bound track to finish an unplanned circumnavigation.

As we set off this time, in a boat that felt downright luxurious compared to 24-foot *Seraffyn*, I still felt twinges of seasickness. In spite of almost a thousand miles of sailing on her, I still had doubts about handling 18,000-pound *Taleisin* in all the situations I knew we'd encounter. I still kept wondering if there was something I forgot to buy. The apprehension I'd had the first time around – worries over handling the problems of entering and living in foreign lands – were gone, but my concerns about storms never completely diminished, so I still found myself checking weather forecasts twice a day at sea, even though I knew we'd just have to deal with the weather as it came our way.

But this first night out I did find the answer to the biggest question that still remained, a question that could not be answered even after our sea trials were finished: would cruising this time be as exciting? The answer came as I climbed out to check our compass course and scan the moon-speckled horizon. Exciting wasn't the correct word this time. Instead, the emotion I felt and recorded in my logbook was: "utter and complete satisfaction." To once again know our preparations were complete, to set off into the organized routine of voyaging away from cities, freeways and time schedules felt good. It's the life we'd chosen. And unlike *Seraffyn*, which we had always thought of as a boat for another six months of cruising, another adventure, *Taleisin* was built to be – and truly felt like – our home.

Early on our second evening out of San Diego, Larry brought up the question which had been hovering at the back of my mind for at least a month. Was it a mistake to start our new voyaging life on the same path as fifteen years before? When *Seraffyn* and I were both untried and untested sailors, a relatively short voyage down the coast of Baja California and leisurely cruise around the Sea of Cortez had been perfect. It had given me a chance to get my sea legs without immediately setting out on a long ocean passage. It had given us a chance to adapt to a cruising lifestyle within a two-week sail of the place we still called home. We'd purposefully kept our cruising goals and plans vague when we spoke to friends so if things didn't work out we could go back and set a different goal with no loss of face. That initial cruise along the shores of Mexico gave us a chance to know *Seraffyn* and grow to trust her in waters that seldom turned stormy. And finally, we'd been able to taste the joys and problems of living with our first foreign culture surrounded and encouraged by some of the most patient people in the world.

But this time, with over 70,000 sea miles behind me, with a tried and tested boat we knew was designed for offshore passagemaking, we didn't really need the easy breaking-in Larry had so wisely chosen for *Seraffyn* and me. Yet Baja California held special memories and seemed the most logical route towards the South Pacific islands. Thus, on the first of November, 1984 we headed for a rendezvous with a land that was like an old friend.

As we sailed down the coast, we couldn't help but wonder: how much has it changed?

Twelve hours after we set sail, when we were well clear of land, we found fresh northerly winds for the 250-mile run from San Diego, just as we had many years before. We'd assumed this new boat, with its extra five feet of waterline, would sail about 20 percent faster than *Seraffyn*. Now we learned that with the extra buoyancy of her flared bow, and the ease with which her more balanced hull steered, we could keep her moving at close to seven knots in complete comfort. So she threw our expected early morning arrival off by making 165 miles the second day out instead of the 115 miles we had always hoped for with *Seraffyn*. We'd had to heave to for most of the night to wait for a safe dawn approach. As the wind increased from a fresh 20 knots to a gusty 35-knot gale, Larry experimented with the balance of mainsail and rudder trim to keep *Taleisin* from tacking through the eye of the wind. Two reefs in the tightly sheeted mainsail and ten degrees of lee helm finally got her lying comfortably. I lay in my bunk feeling the same sick headache and urge to vomit I'd felt within 20 miles of this same spot so many years before. But this time I knew I'd get better and forget the discomfort as soon as we lay at anchor.

We had fond memories of the mariachis whose music we'd come to love during our previous visits to Baja California and mainland Mexico. We were not disappointed this time around.

The first time we sailed into the lee of Isla Guadalupe we hadn't taken note of the mantle of cloud creeping over the island. This time, with much more experience behind us, we were prepared for the strong williwaws it foretold.

As we ran beneath the high cliffs of Guadalupe the next morning, 50-knot williwaws raked the waters of the bay just as they had many years ago. But this time they didn't take us by surprise – though the heavy swell running through the anchorage where we'd laid relatively comfortably on *Seraffyn* did. So we sailed onward, skirting the unchanging, barren shores of this lonely Mexican outpost. Colonies of elephant seals and sea lions still littered the rocky ledges. Only a few isolated fishermen's shacks could be seen until we rounded to the southern end of the island where a fish camp and small army detachment huddled near the only other possible anchorage on this sheer-sided island. We found a sheltered spot in eight fathoms of water, just before dark. But by morning a southerly swell began sweeping into the open roadstead. The wind still blew from the north, but the weather report we picked up by tuning our short wave receiver to WWV Fort Collins Colorado told of a late hurricane situated 800 miles south of us and lying almost stationary. That explained these three-foot swells breaking against the cliffs 300 yards in front of us.

Three Mexican fishermen hailed us soon after we heard this report. With the same easy joking we remembered from years before, they convinced us to stay for a day.

"The waves, they will lay down tomorrow. Then you can come and have beer with us. You want some lobster? We'll get you some, just wait."

Thirty minutes later they were back. They carefully maneuvered their rough-looking eighteen-foot work boat alongside, fending off as *Taleisin* rolled in the surge, then dumped seven live lobsters onto our deck.

"How much do you want for these?" I asked.

"Nothing," called two of the men. "A present for you. We have too many."

The third man asked, "Do you have any American beer?"

Larry found the only beer we had on board – a six-pack of Coors. After urging us to come ashore the next day, they headed off. I watched through binoculars as the fishermen timed the breaking three-foot swells to land their open boat safely on a rocky ramp.

By the next morning the swells were even heavier. Even with the ersatz flopper-stopper, created using our 20-foot-long spinnaker pole and a canvas bucket weighted down with 30 feet of spare anchor chain, we were beginning to roll almost gunnel to gunnel. It was frustrating to be so close to warm, welcoming folks yet feel so threatened and separated by the pounding surf. We remembered the interesting conversations we'd had with fishermen just like these long before on this same isolated and lonely island. The gifts they'd asked us to deliver to families on the mainland had opened many doors for us. But each time we listened to the radio weather update, the hurricane center seemed to be creeping ever so slowly towards us, its track perfect to keep sending long rolling swells across the miles to make the anchorage of Guadalupe increasingly less safe. So after two days of rolling, waiting and hoping, we lifted anchor and ran out from the lee of Guadalupe, bound for Turtle Bay, one of the most unsightly villages in Baja California.

We'd never come here with *Seraffyn*. But we had stopped at the village of Turtle Bay (Bahia Tortuga) a half dozen times when we were delivering different boats up this barren coastline. Until recently we'd anchored near the fish cannery dominated village only long enough to buy fuel, get a night's sleep then move onward. Two months before we departed from San Diego on board *Taleisin*, we'd heard about a terrible incident that occurred in this isolated place. Two American cruising sailors had been killed by an escaped American convict. The wife of one was tortured, her boat stolen then put on the rocks at the entrance to the bay. She got back to San Diego bereft and broke, with her boat sitting exposed to the hurricanes. We'd volunteered to rescue the boat for her and, with the help of some of the Turtle Bay's inhabitants, we were able to repair and sail the boat back to San Diego, though it had been a bit more of an adventure than we expected.[1]

The stark red and beige desert surrounding the village overwhelmed the bit of green provided by the dusty, rugged pinyon trees villagers struggled to keep alive in this desolate corner of one of the driest deserts on the American continent. The only drinking water for the village of almost 2000 people came from two desalination machines that hummed 24 hours a day just 200 feet from the restless surge of the sea. At first glance there was almost nothing to relieve the bleakness of drifting red dust except the bright blues and greens many villagers used to paint the fronts of their tiny stucco or adobe houses. Not a tree, nor patch of grass. That's probably why, as I walked through the village the next day, I noticed a tiny garden tucked behind a protective fence next to where two men happily pounded away on an old pickup truck, trying to straighten fenders that were more rust than metal.

"Whose garden is this? " I asked one of them using the Spanish originally gained during our first visit to Mexico on *Seraffyn*.

"It is my wife's folly," he answered. Then he began telling me how she wasted time carrying buckets of water to each of two dozen flowering bushes.

"Do you think she would sell me some of the flowers to have on my boat?"

The man didn't answer. He ran off shouting, "Maria, Maria, a lady from the yacht likes your flowers!"

Maria came strutting out from behind the house.

"See Juan, flowers are important too," she said as she began picking purple blooms from a rugged bush.

I tried to stop her from denuding her garden, saying my vases were only tiny hanging ones. But my protest came to no avail. She carefully arranged the huge bundle of flowers as if she were a professional florist. Then her "I told you so" look softened as Juan came out of the house with a red ribbon to secure the bouquet. I watched him take Maria's hand as I offered to pay.

"A gift," they both said in unison. "We'll see you at the big dinner this afternoon. The food will be great."

We stopped to buy four lobsters for the equivalent of $1 US each at a small stall in front of another house.

After the stall's owner finished admiring our bouquet and tried to

1 We recount this story and the lessons it taught us in *The Capable Cruiser.*

refuse payment for her husband's catch, she said, "Don't eat too much now. There will be lots of food for you later."

When the old man lounging on the pier next to our dinghy said, "See you at the big dance," we finally asked, "What dinner, what dance?"

"Why, the 28th anniversary celebration of our fishing co-op," he said, proudly pointing to a banner that stretched 100 feet across the heavily weathered, unpainted concrete building at the head of the pier.

Four hours later we cautiously joined the crowd heading towards a low-slung building at the edge of the town. We didn't have a chance to remain shy. People pulled us inside the gym/community center building, where they cleared a space on a littered table. Soon brandy, beer, bottles of cola and plates full of boiled potatoes, salad, stewed beef, beans and fresh handmade tortillas appeared from huge platters and cauldrons at the back of the 100-foot-long hall. A five-piece band blared out Latin tunes as we ate. Dogs scampered at our feet; youngsters tried their high school English on us and told us how their town was the very best town in Mexico. Twenty minutes later a squad of boisterous, energetic men began disassembling tables and dumping everything on the floor: beer bottles, plates, half-eaten tortillas. A dozen women appeared at the front of the hall with wide brooms and began moving purposefully in a line towards the rear, shoving trash, dogs, kids and anyone who stood in front of them. A pickup truck arrived behind the building just in time to receive the piles of party waste and, less than five minutes after the feast ended, the dance floor was miraculously clean.

At least 300 people danced and gossiped, showed us their babies and posed for photos while children played games around their feet. We felt confused at times, trying to keep up with their questions, working to remember words of Spanish we hadn't used in years. But we felt comfortable and welcome as we danced together to music that often had an American melody but Latin beat.

Larry asked me to go for a stroll outside when the dancing and press of the crowd began to make us sweat. We walked a half block to stand on the cliff overlooking the bay. A huge moon began to rise among the rugged desert mesas and trackless wastes to the east just as the sunset turned the sand of the beach a rosy bronze and the water of the bay a vivid emerald green. A woman walked from her house just behind us and came to stand a few feet from where Larry and I watched this awe-inspiring sight.

When the moon rose above the hills we turned to leave, the woman smiled and said, "Don't you agree? I live in the most beautiful place in the world."

The setting sun casting its golden glow across Turtle Bay, the rising moon adding a silver tinge to the crests of the desert hills; in this light it was indeed beautiful.

When we set sail a week later we knew the lobster lady by her name. Consuelo. We'd been invited to her daughter's sweet fifteen party. Consuelo raved about the hair ribbons we'd found in my sewing supplies as a birthday gift for her daughter, the crisp green apples we'd brought to add to the birthday feast. We'd seen Juan's final paint job on the vastly restored pickup truck and gotten to know each tiny shop and fruit stand in the fifteen-square-block town. We'd also come to admire these tough people who battled a constant film of desert dust and dryness, who lived with the isolation of being 125 miles from the nearest town, which could only be reached by driving over a rutted dirt track then across tire-lacerating salt pans, yet managed to make their town seem beautiful.

Amazingly, we found no change at all in places like Bahia Santa Maria, where we had to weave our way past three dozing whales to reach the anchorage which we shared with two fish boats. And later in the Gulf of California in each place where there were no towns, we saw the same itinerant fishermen's shacks hidden in protected corners of isolated bays. Though often shy at first, these hard-working men were just as willing to share their stories, tortillas and catch as had been the fishermen we'd met in these same places fifteen years before. The same stunningly desolate landscapes greeted each glowing sunset. The same black rock mountains towered over brilliantly colored sandscapes in sharp contrast to the pastel greens and vivid blues of the tropical warm sea. Like before, the almost breathtaking scenic views made me wish I could somehow capture this beauty with paint and brush.

The beauty of the place was not the only thing that was familiar. The same 20- to 25-knot northwesterly winds sent ten-foot swells breaking against the sandy shores of Baja California to make beating north inside the gulf hard work.

The guardian rocks that protect Cabo San Lucas from the omnipresent northwest Pacific swells must surely be changing as the wind and water grind year after year against them. But we could see no difference. On shore, however, the change was stunning. Where only one hotel overlooked the open bay some years back, now a half dozen seemed to have grown from the rocks and sand. Where a rough dirt airstrip used to welcome sportfishing clients in front of the Hacienda Hotel only 200 yards from the water's edge, a dredged harbor now offered complete protection for over 100 yachts plus the large ferry that runs from here to Mexico's mainland. The sleepy Mexican village of 800 people we had once known had been completely engulfed by tourism. When we arrived to anchor off the beach, we soon learned almost 15,000 Mexicans work to provide luxuries for many thousand North Americans who come here as tourists or as retirees to enjoy the crystal-clear waters, warm breezes and exciting sportfishing. We soon came to feel Cabo San Lucas was no longer really Mexican; now it was more like an American's version of what Mexico should be.

But the local postmaster shared his view a few days after we arrived.

"When I was a boy growing up here, this was just a tiny fishing village that starved one year and just survived the next," he said. "Now many of us have real opportunities. I have been able to send two of my boys to the university in Mexico City and many of our children can find real work, not just selling chewing gum on street corners or offering to polish shoes for a few pennies at a time. That isn't so in many of the other fishing villages."

We had a great time in Cabo San Lucas the first time we visited it. In spite of all the changes, we enjoyed the second time too, but our pleasures were less rustic. We humbled ourselves by renting surf-sailing boards from a concession stand on the beach. I sailed a few hundred yards then crashed, tried again and cursed until exhaustion took over. Larry did better, actually sailing a quarter mile at a time.

But as we rowed wearily back towards *Taleisin* he nodded in agreement

It was near Cabo San Lucas that we met first met Mike Kris on his 34-foot Gilpie, *a 1938 wooden ketch he sailed several times across the Pacific.*

when I said, "Next time I'll take lessons before I set off on one of those things."

Then there was the evening we joined ten other cruising sailors at a highly recommended "tourist" restaurant, *El Coralle*, for a dinner of perfectly barbequed Sonora beef that rivaled any Texas steaks I've eaten. Margaritas, freshly made, silky-textured flour tortillas and spicy ceviche reminded us we *were* in Mexico, even if the fine recordings of Verdi operas seemed a bit out of place. We savored the warm, almost sultry evening. Then all of us rowed across the harbor to lounge on the elegant balcony of the Hacienda Hotel where, for the cost of a drink, we could rub shoulders with hotel guests who paid up to $1500 US a night. Los Lobos, a seven-piece Mariachi band that entertained us over the next three hours, was the finest I've heard. Larry and I danced together to the strains of *Spanish Eyes* then one of the trumpet players jumped in as a willing partner when I tried to do a Mexican Hat Dance. The highlight of evening came as we all grew heavy-eyed and began to say our farewells. The Mariachis seemed to disperse when suddenly, from the far out near the sea, we heard the call of a lone trumpet. From somewhere deep in the halls of the hotel another trumpet seemed to answer in the sweetest, saddest tones I've ever heard. The nine remaining members of the group strolled over to where we sat and played a more upbeat chorus. Then we again heard the two trumpets crying to each other across the hotel grounds, though they sounded just a bit closer.

"El Niño Perdido," whispered the waiter who came to clear our table. "The song of the lost child."

Slowly the trumpets came closer and closer until they joined the two violins and the guitars in the joyful reunion of parents and child. Only then did we leave, walking across the sand towards where our dinghy lay waiting. The quiet of the night was broken only by the wavelets that burbled along the shore. Neither of us said a word, but I knew Larry too was thinking of the wonderful contrasts that kept our lives so full.

Within a few hours of anchoring at Cabo San Lucas, we'd been hailed by Pete Sutter, a retired sailmaker and well-known racing sailor from Sausalito. We'd met at his sail loft two years previously and when Pete told us of his plan to retire and set off voyaging, Larry had jokingly said, "We'll have *Taleisin* finished and ready to go before then, so let's meet for Thanksgiving 1984 at Cabo San Lucas."

Pete had taken him seriously. "The turkey is arriving in an hour, so we'll have a proper Thanksgiving dinner for you in two days," Pete called. "Anne is flying in with all the fixings."

The dinner she prepared for eight of us on board their Wylie designed 38-foot fast cruiser *Wild Spirit* had all of the expected American delights, plus local delicacies. The conversation ranged far and wide, with Larry and Pete having to be guided away from the technicalities of fast sail shapes and boat design details. But what caught our attention were Pete's cruising plans.

During our years on *Seraffyn*, we'd voyaged east-about, never once going south of the equator. So it was here at Cabo that, for the first time, we found ourselves surrounded by cruising sailors bound towards the tradewinds and tropical islands along the "Milk Run." We knew there were a lot more folks out voyaging now and weren't surprised to find almost five times the number we'd met at anchor here when we first started voyaging. The size of boats had jumped too. Where in 1970 the average length of the fourteen other cruising boats that shared this anchorage had been about 29 feet, now the boats around us probably averaged closer to 38 feet in length and a much smaller percentage had been built by their owners. But what surprised us most was the number of people who, as soon as we met, told us they were headed around the world with a defined number

A mid-afternoon wash-down helps keep the decks feeling cool. The salt and moisture also help preserve the teak and keep the timber from drying out and shrinking, and the deck from leaking.

of years set aside for their voyage.

Larry and I talked late into the night about this, comparing this to the attitude that had prevailed – or so it seemed to us – in years past. Then we enjoyed, along with other voyagers, a kind of "isn't it great just to be out cruising for more than a three- or four-week holiday" approach – one that conveyed an easy-going "let's take one day at a time, wander where the wind blows us" attitude.

"I wonder if these folks realize the pressure they're putting on themselves," Larry said as we took a break from socializing. "What if they really like a place and want to stay a while, or if someone invites them to a great destination that lies in a completely different direction? And what if they find they don't like crossing oceans, or being pushed on by the season. Now they've told everyone what their plans are, they'll feel like they're losers if they don't make it all the way. But, they all seem so locked into their round-the-world schedules."

That evening we learned Pete had this same goal, with a three-year, port-by-port plan laid out and promises from various friends to join him at places that sounded interesting or romantic along his route. As New Zealand was on his itinerary, we knew we'd share other anchorages along the first legs of his voyage. This delighted both of us as we'd found we had a lot in common, especially with our mutual enjoyment of pure sailing spiced by occasional races. But we secretly worried over Pete's planned circumnavigation, and wondered how he'd fare being on such a strict itinerary.

And then, Pete's plans changed. About nine months into his intended round-the-world voyage, Pete happened to stop at an out-of-the way island in Fiji. There he met a group of Kiribati people from an island which had been almost completely destroyed by a British phosphate mining company. The company had bought an uninhabited island from the Fijians and provided transport and some basic housing to resettle the Kiribatis. Unfortunately, these people, whose existence was dependent on fishing, using sailing canoes, had spent their lives very close to the equator where light winds are the norm. They were not prepared for the heavier winds they encountered at their new island home. Their flour sack sails were not strong enough; they had no funds to buy stronger fabrics. Pete had a few old sails on board and a sewing machine. Soon he had outfitted several of the canoes with sails more suited to the local conditions. Of course he became an immediate hero. But helping a few people was not enough; soon Pete had a mission. He sailed down to New Zealand and started collecting good used sails – and for the next three years he sailed between Fiji and New Zealand or Australia each year.

When we were last together in Australia, he brought up the conversations we'd had four years previously in Cabo San Lucas.

"You guys had it right," Pete said. "And now I tell everyone the same thing – even though I had to re-arrange all the dates I made with my sailing buddies before I left Sausalito, it was far, far better that I wasn't too pig-headed to change my plans. I'm really glad I got stuck in the Pacific eddy – otherwise I would have missed the very best years of my life."

I think it was only when we left Cabo San Lucas to sail northward into the Sea of Cortez and approached the Cerralvo Channel that I began to fully trust the windvane Larry had created for us. Though he had assured me it was just a modification of the successful vane we'd used on *Seraffyn*, it looked and felt different to me. But he was right: it picked up every wind shift as we beat northward, kept steering true even when winds dropped to less than five knots. Just as important, as we battled the choppy seas and gusty winds, I began to appreciate the 6600 pounds of ballast that made up almost 40 percent of *Taleisin*'s total cruising weight. When we'd made this same 120-mile voyage on lightly ballasted *Seraffyn* (she carried only 26 percent of her total cruising weight in the lead ballast keel) it had been a five-day odyssey as we tried to punch into the short, steep head seas. Each night we'd sheltered behind any headland we could, licking our wounds, sneaking out early each morning in the hopes the winds might be lighter, the seas easier to handle. But *Taleisin*'s extra ballast and her longer buttocks helped her drive to windward under full working sail in 24 knots of wind, and kept her moving at close to six knots. Whenever the wind dropped a knot or two, we set the staysail to keep her powering onward. When the wind increased again, we dropped her staysail. Through the night she charged along as we took one long tack to seaward of Cerralvo Island, a route that was 50 miles longer than we'd taken our first time here. And our windvane, which swung incongruously around the backstay, picked up every wind shift to keep us gaining to windward, lifting *Taleisin*'s bow ever closer to our rhumb line course as the wind backed from north-northwest to northwest. Only 24 hours after we left Cabo San Lucas we were able to tack over and clear La Foca Reef, just north of Cerralvo Island, then reach through the San Lorenzo Channel and turn south to run towards our favorite Mexican town, La Paz.

It was relatively easy for friends and family to fly down and join in when we were cruising in the Sea of Cortez. Lauren and Mike (who took the photo that opens this chapter) explored the waters north of La Paz with us.

Taleisin has two antique crystal hanging vases, one to port next to the chart table, the other to starboard next to the galley. Though I prefer fresh flowers, like many of the homemakers of Baja California where water is scarce and live flowers even more so, I became a client of the artificial flower seller.

We'd spent almost six months cruising on *Seraffyn* within 50 miles of the capital of Baja California del Sur. Our memories were stirred by each mountain peak and each bay we sailed past. Within a day of arriving, we'd been recognized and welcomed by a half dozen Mexican people we'd known fifteen years before. So even though the city had doubled in population, even though more than 50 yachts lay anchored where eight had been before, we still were able to find our favorite taco stand, our favorite café.

Nevil Shute, one of my favorite authors, once wrote, "You can only do something for the first time once." Our voyage down the coast of Baja California proved that to us. No longer did we have the thrills and spills of trying to figure out our first bits of Spanish. No longer did each entry to each bay seem like an adventure. Yet our decision to return to Baja California had not been a mistake. As we'd found before, it is still a perfect place to start a cruise: close enough to home so we could invite some of our family and special friends to join us to sample our cruising life; wild and isolated enough so we could do a final test of our equipment before we set off across an ocean; foreign enough to prove we'd actually made the final break.

Now we were truly cruising.

The man-of-war, or greater frigate birds, were always on the lookout when the shrimping boats of Baja were pulling in their nets. In a way we were little different, watching for the shrimpers to anchor near us then rowing over to trade fresh cookies or some beer for a bucket of shrimp.

It took only a day to fall into the pleasant routine of sea-going. Note the very useful shoulder-high lifeline we add when we head out to sea.

CHAPTER 4

BETWEEN WHALE TALES

With 2000 miles of California sea trials and easy Baja California cruising behind her, *Taleisin* could no longer be called a new boat. We'd tested her power as we beat north against 25- and 30-knot winds to re-visit the magic hideaways of the Gulf of California. As we explored the hidden coves we'd prowled around sixteen years before on *Seraffyn* and raced against new and old friends in the tranquil waters of the Bay of La Paz, we'd found the best leads for our light-air sails. A few fresh reaches had forced me to re-arrange lockers so I could actually get at the provisions I wanted even when I wasn't feeling my very best. So now, as we left Cabo San Lucas headed south and west, bound for the Marquesas, *Taleisin* was in top sailing shape, though she was loaded well beyond her 17,400-pound-designed sailing displacement. In fact, a check of her waterline marks showed her ready-to-depart weight was close to 18,600 pounds. But everything was hidden in its proper locker, other than four baskets of fresh, fragrant fruit and vegetables which we'd wedged securely at the head of the forward bunk.

Ahead of us now lay a whole new world. In eighteen years of voyaging

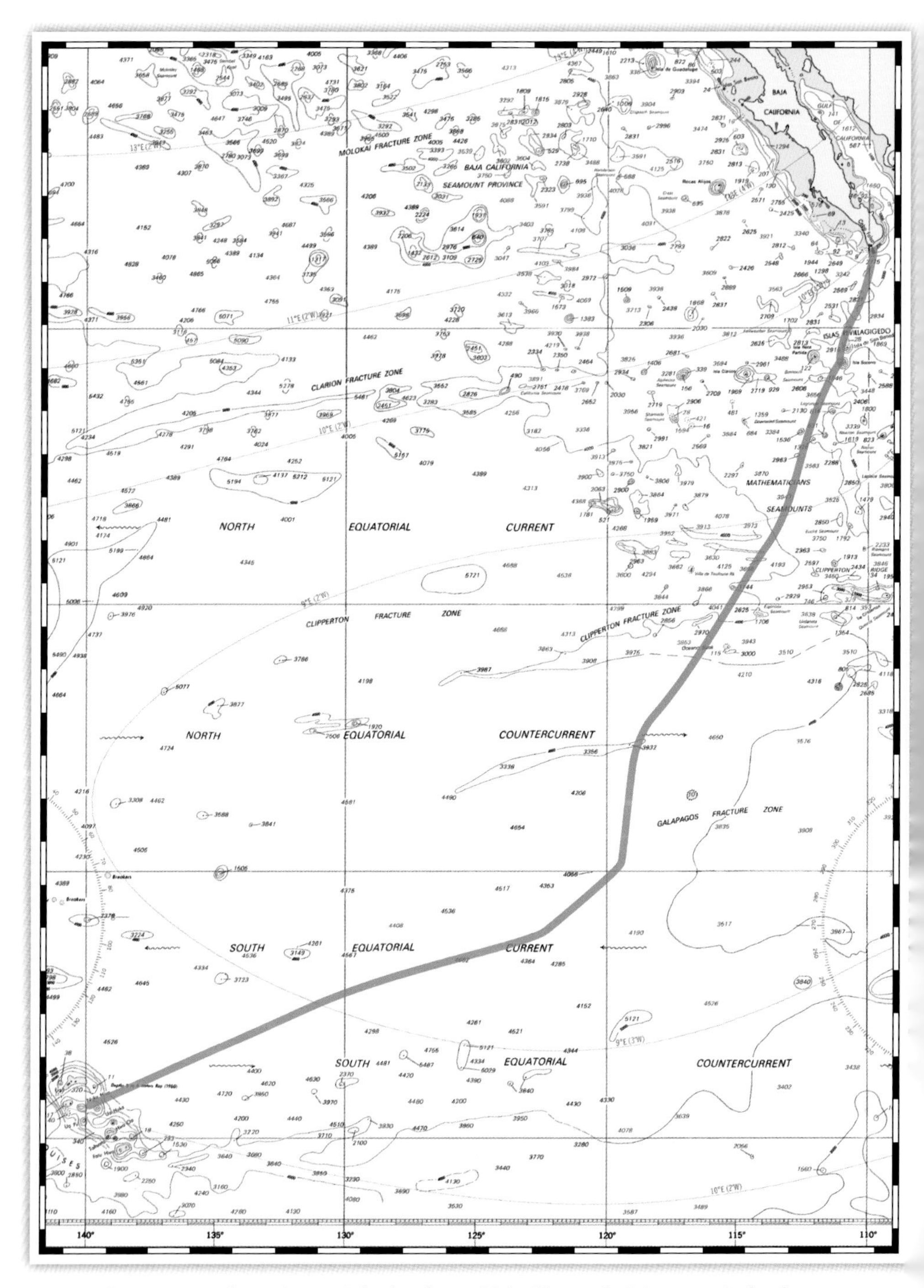

Our course south past Socorro Island and on to Nuka Hiva in the Marquesas Archipelago. The jog in our route took us through the narrowest part of the ITCZ.

we'd never once poked our bowsprit south of the equator, never visited a South Seas island or coral atoll, never heard the throbbing drums of Polynesia.

Two days' sailing south of Cabo San Lucas lies Socorro Island. Rugged, desolate, it is inhabited on shore only by a small contingent of Mexican soldiers. Under water it is reputed to be haven to the largest spiny lobster population in the Pacific. We planned to stop for a few days to frolic amid the underwater denizens and secure a few good feeds of what Larry and I consider to be one of the finest delicacies in the world (those from Maine still argue their true lobster is better but…), before setting off for the long haul to Polynesia.

It was late morning when we reached in towards Socorro's only tenable anchorage, an open bay tucked tightly against the southwest corner of the island and shielded from the prevailing winds and swells by protecting arms of rock. The water within the bay didn't look right. I got out the binoculars and could now make out wispy plumes of spray, then the slowly arching backs of seven grey whales as they stirred the waters by moving in a slow pavane, circling the only shoal area we could safely use. We dropped the lapper (equivalent to a number 3 genoa) and, under staysail and main, reached closer.

Larry reassured me, "They'll leave any second now. Besides, they're probably farther offshore than they look from this angle. We'll sail in past them and have lots of room to anchor."

He was wrong on all counts. The placid, obviously amorous behemoths ignored us completely as we slowly reached alongside them and carried on with their mating activities. I threw the leadline to sound the anchorage; they still didn't leave. In fact, the closer we got, the more they seemed to fill the anchorage. They seemed to fill every bit of space, swimming to within a dozen yards of the shore with their massive, heaving, barge-like bodies.

We gybed, then reached clear of the anchorage, and as the full swell of the open ocean again caught us I said, "Let's forget Socorro – wind's fair, let's keep going."

But Larry's eyes got their mad hunter look. "Remember what that Mexican diver told us about the lobster here. I can't wait to slip into the water and grab a few. Probably never have another feed as good as the one we'll have tonight."

So we winched in the main and staysail sheets, tacked over and left the staysail backed. *Taleisin* slowly lost way and lay comfortably hove-to while I made lunch. Two hours later we eased the staysail sheet to turn and reach back in to the anchorage. By then, our harbor mates had moved –

somewhat. Now there was *almost* enough room for us to set our anchor as the whales nuzzled around each other, rolling body-to-body against each other, completely ignoring us. But not quite enough. So we gybed and reached out into the open water again, to lay hove-to for another hour. Then we sailed in yet again. The necking-party-cum-gossip session seemed less intimate now as the whales swam in three separate groups. Amidst them there appeared to be just enough swinging room to set our anchor and let out chain to equal just four times the waters depth. Before I could change my mind, Larry had unclutched the anchor windlass and eased out our 35-pound CQR with 150 feet of chain.

Our big grey cove mates ignored the rattling chain but acquiesced to our territorial claim, swimming and cavorting just clear of *Taleisin*. I turned to Larry.

"Going in for some fresh dinner fixings? I'll get out your fins."

My urgings, done in jest, were ignored. He sat next to me on the cabin top, watching those whales, imagining the teeming sea life crawling through the crevices and crannies of the sea-washed rocks just 200 yards from where we lay at anchor. That evening, as we chewed our way through some durable Mexican chicken and braced ourselves against the slight surge in the anchorage, the whale-induced wavelets and occasional gusts of the fresh westerly breezes scooting down from the hills inshore of us, Larry said, "I'll slip overboard and chase up a bug or two tomorrow, when our friends move on."

By morning it was we who decided to move on – to get a good night's rest by going to sea. The serenade of whale spouting, augmented by what we took to be sighs of sexual delight, kept us both on the edge of wakefulness through the night. The whales acknowledged our departure by immediately filling the gap we left as we sailed slowly from the anchorage. Within an hour we were free of the wind-shadow of Socorro Island and gliding over a sun-speckled sea, three sails set to catch the fifteen-knot westerly, fishing line set to catch a mahi mahi, or at least something fishy and fresh to augment our limited supply of Mexican meat.

The wind slowly eased from our beam then across our stern until we were running wing and wing in the northeasterly trades. The only comments worth recording in our log, other than course and distance made good, were: "*Baked bread, had a hot shower, took cushions out onto the foredeck for the afternoon, made love in the shade of the drifter.*"

As I read that comment, the scene floods back in warm details: the green and blue striped sail arching over us, providing a perfect screen from the tropical sun; the smell of fresh bread slowly baking below decks, wafting up through the open forehatch; the sound of Earl Klug's guitar carrying softly from our stereo, his strumming almost in perfect rhythm with the hiss, then gurgle, as *Taleisin*'s bow rode over the crest of each surging wave.

For once I truly believed perfect trade wind sailing existed. We'd found it and *Taleisin* loved it. The string of noon-to-noon runs recorded in our log belied her relatively small size: 158, 165, 176, the current giving us a few extra miles on top of that. The days sped past in the easy going, intimate routine that seems to develop on board a two-handed sailboat during an ocean passage.

Keeping the necessary round-the-clock watch means Larry and I find we spend little time actually being together when we are at sea. Three hours on, three hours off all night, our only communications being a quick update from the person coming off-watch. "Lovely sailing, eased the pole forward a bit, no chafe on the sheets, had some dolphins come by," would be a typical comment from Larry as he climbed into the bunk.

Larry was amazingly chipper coming off watch. As the still-groggy new watch person, I'd try to be polite at the same time, wishing Larry would shut up and go to sleep. Three hours later and the roles were reversed: Larry was now the groggy one, me animated and talkative as I nestled into the still warm bunk. We each then spent two hours napping later in the day to top up our need for about eight hours' sleep each day. Then there was the time needed to make occasional sail changes, navigate, clean up inside the boat, check the gear on deck, check the fresh produce for signs of deterioration. With only the two of us on board, we find that at sea we have less than four hours of unstructured time for cooking, eating, communications. If one or the other of us happens to be fully engrossed in reading the concluding chapters of a book we "just can't put down," we find our only true time together happens as we share our evening meal then begin the routine of lighting and filling the oil navigation lamps, settling the boat for the night, then having a quiet drink, a quick sing-along or a shared chapter from a book we might choose to read aloud together before Larry climbs into the bunk.

Bobbie McGee left her lover a dozen times, the drunken sailor suffered a hundred insults and the Fox Went Hunting almost every day as Larry and I sang through our limited repertoire and Taleisin rushed southward.

As on all previous passages, we stuck to our routine of having the same watches each night on this first crossing from Mexico to Polynesia. Studies by sleep psychologists confirm what we have learned by trial and error. Our body clocks adjust more quickly to sleeping during the same time periods each night instead of dogging or alternating watch hours as is the custom on boats with larger crews. By the third night of any passage we are able to fall quickly to sleep, to wake with reasonable alacrity at the end of each watch. But if we dog the watches we find our sleep patterns disturbed all through the passage.

Two things began to indicate the unique nature of this passage. First, not one of our night watches was interrupted by a call for assistance. In fact, due to the lovely sailing conditions, the person on watch was able to make the few nighttime sail adjustments so quietly that every off-watch was an uninterrupted flow of wave-lulled dreams. The second oddity: by our tenth day out from Socorro we hadn't found the doldrums which should have slowed our progress well before we reached the equator. In fact, when our sun and star sights showed a current against us – a sure sign of the edge of the doldrums – the seas steadied and the wind shifted just enough to put us on our fastest point of sail, a beam reach. Now *Taleisin* with her 27'6" waterline turned in a wondrous series of noon to noon runs: 168, 176, 171. Our taffrail log reading and celestial sights concurred to within a mile or two to rule out help from stray currents.

As exciting as this was, it presented a new problem.

Both of us are fair-skinned. Though neither of us could be called sun-worshipers, many years of enjoying sailing before medical science made the link between sun exposure and skin cancers meant we'd both acquired a fair sprinkling of keratosis (the early stages of sun-induced skin cancer). These scaly patches and re-occurring small lesions had, in the past, been frozen off or surgically removed during a visit to the doctor's office. But our personal physician didn't like the scars these methods left and suggested an alternative – a chemical treatment which, after giving us careful instructions, he felt we could use on our own. We'd previously tried this treatment under his direction, applying Efudex[1] twice daily for three weeks, watching the sun spots redden, and then turn to open sores then scab over and heal, leaving amazingly smooth, blemish-free skin behind. The spots we'd treated under the doctor's supervision had all been on our forearms and easily hidden from public view by Band-Aids. Now the affected areas were on our faces. We kept putting off the treatment, waiting for a time when we'd be away from people for a while. The time seemed right on this longer passage. Just before we set sail from Mexico I measured the distance we had to sail.

"It's more than 2500 miles to the Marquesas," I'd said to Larry. "We'll be at sea for three weeks or more. If we start the treatment a day or two before we leave, our skin will be all cleared up before we get there."

But by our thirteenth day at sea, when another 158-mile noon-to-noon

1 Efudex is made by Roche Ltd. It is basically chemotherapy for the skin using fluorouracil cream.

run, put us within 400 miles of Nuka Hiva. I looked at Larry splotched countenance, then took a mirror to inspect my own ravaged face and knew we'd made a slight miscalculation. Both of us looked like refugees from a fire. Dozens of red sores lay scattered across my forehead and cheeks, and there were only signs of the first scabs forming. Unless we shortened sail drastically or hove-to for a few days, we'd arrive looking almost leprous.

There is a saying among sailors: "Put one sailboat within sight of another and both will start racing." There wasn't another boat within hundreds of miles of us. But the splendid record of miles made good was as much of a prod as the sight of another sail on the horizon. So, in spite of our appearances, we kept *Taleisin* running as fast as she could, drifter held to one side by the 20-foot spinnaker pole, mainsail to the other, secured with our combination vang/preventer, using winds that only for one day blew over 20 knots.

Speed and steady, satisfying sailing beat vanity. It was really no contest.

Fifteen days out, Larry broke our quiet routine to take a round of five evening stars to confirm our position before our actual landfall. On the morning of the sixteenth day at sea, the craggy outline of our first South Seas island seemed to burst over the horizon. *Taleisin* surged down the trade wind swells as the sheer black cliffs of Nuka Hiva slid ever closer. The fish line we'd been trailing for almost 2400 miles sprang to life, sounding the alarm Larry had jury-rigged by putting a couple of nuts and bolts inside an empty beer tin, then hanging it from a shock cord at the inboard end of the line.

Larry almost trampled me as he rushed through the cockpit to grab the 100-pound test monofilament line. A gold-fringed tuna leapt into the air, skidding and turning behind us, growing ever more frantic as Larry pulled it hand-over-hand towards the boat, then flipped it over the lifelines. I ran as far out of the way of that flailing flash of silver as I could, clinging to the fish-free safety of the boom gallows until it was subdued. My screams of "Kill it before it jumps down the hatch!" died in my throat as a strange black smoothness disturbed the crest of the swell ahead of *Taleisin*. The next ten-foot swell lifted *Taleisin*'s stern and sent her scudding downhill amidst a burst of foam, guided only by the windvane self-steering gear. She seemed to hang motionless for just a few seconds in the trough of the sea as I pointed in stunned silence. Less than ten feet away on our beam, two huge whales lay side by side, gently spouting, basking serenely, probably asleep in the warm tropical sun, unaware that only fate had kept nine tons of rushing timber and lead from landing on their backs.

"Luck, only luck. That's all that kept us from a real catastrophe," Larry whispered as he held the slowly dying eight-pound tuna against the leeward bulwark rail with his foot.

My mind was whirling, filled with visions of a massive, angry fluke smashing through our teak planking, driven by 20 tons of terrified mammal. From the look in Larry's eyes I could tell he was recalling another encounter with sleeping whales almost eighteen years before when he'd been first mate on an 85-foot schooner, the *Double Eagle*. He'd been at the helm when, halfway between Hawaii and California, they'd sailed quietly past a basking whale. One of the crew tossed an empty beer can at the mammal. Its frenzied dive had sent cascades of salt water right across the massive schooner to drench the crew both on deck and below under the open companionway hatch.

"If that fluke had hit our stem, it would have shattered it," Larry had often told me.

Now we watched in silence as, astern, white wavelets washed across the backs of the whales. *Taleisin* lifted and fled before another trade wind

Larry noticed the staysail halyard was showing signs of chafe . So one day, when the sails where pulling well and holding the boat relatively steady, he went aloft and found the problem. We added an anti-chafing guard below the halyard block soon after we arrived in the Marquesas.

swell, and within two minutes those whales were lost from view. The smells of approaching land slowly invaded my senses. A last death thump from the fish Larry was still holding under his foot brought him out of his shock-induced trance. We were soon occupied with fish filets, sail changes, navigation. Neither of us mentioned our close encounter with those mammoth creatures that shared this water with us until we lay in our bunk together late that evening.

It was dark when we short-tacked between the towering sides of Taihoe Bay and shattered the quiet with the rattle of our anchor chain. The gentle beat up the bay had let us savor the special sounds of shore life: the call of night birds, the croak of land frogs, the sweetness of a villager on shore singing a few lines of a song that was completely new to us. Sixteen days, six hours out of Socorro we lay at anchor after a passage that could be described as close to perfection.

Morning brought reality with it.

At the first sight of our yellow quarantine flag, the health officer arrived. One look at our sore-encrusted faces and he informed us we were confined on board until further notice. Our attempts to use our 20-word French vocabulary failed completely. But he did take our tube of Efudex with him and he did make it clear he would be contacting the authorities in Papeete, Tahiti, for further instructions. It was late afternoon before he returned, accompanied by customs officials and immigration officials,

plus the postmaster – who carried a bottle of wine to officially welcome us and invite us to explore his island home.

An old sailing friend once said, "You'll go out sailing ten times, then you'll hit one day that is sheer magic. You'll be hooked and go out again and again trying to fall under that intoxicating spell once more."

When I looked back at all the voyaging we'd done *on Seraffyn*, the passages we'd made delivering other people's boats, I had to agree with his sentiment: truly memorable days were vastly outnumbered by those days when sailing was merely pleasant, or other days that were utterly mundane, or hard work or even downright difficult. I knew this would be the case as we voyaged onward. But now, on *Taleisin*, the difficult and stormy days as well as the mundane days would be set against the memory of our highly satisfying dash, neatly sandwiched between two whale tales, from Mexico to the South Pacific.

Cheeky, *with her sailing rig, provided endless hours of pleasure for us and for youngsters we met along the way. We also carried a small outboard which could push her along at four knots. For skin diving we had an inflatable collar which made her very stable and easy to board directly from the water.*

Chapter 5

The Pleasure in Madness

"No rocks, no outcroppings along here," I tell Larry as we row within an oar's length of the cliff face. "We could tack right in close here."

"Yes, but seems as if this cliff sucks up the wind," Larry answers. "With this surge rolling along it, I'd hate to try tacking and end up in irons. Let's row out just a bit past the point, see if the wind will give us a lift or a header there."

Twenty minutes later we head back to *Taleisin* and begin stowing her sun cover.

As we go about the now familiar routine of preparing to get under way Larry says, "Here's how I figure it: we reach down towards the entrance, head up close to the wind and take a few practice tacks. If we aren't comfortable we bail out, come back and anchor to wait another day. Wind might shift further to the east, trades might ease off. But I think we can make it out if we get up a head of steam and beat in as close as we dare to the cliff, then we tack and if all goes to well we should be to windward enough to be clear of that point."

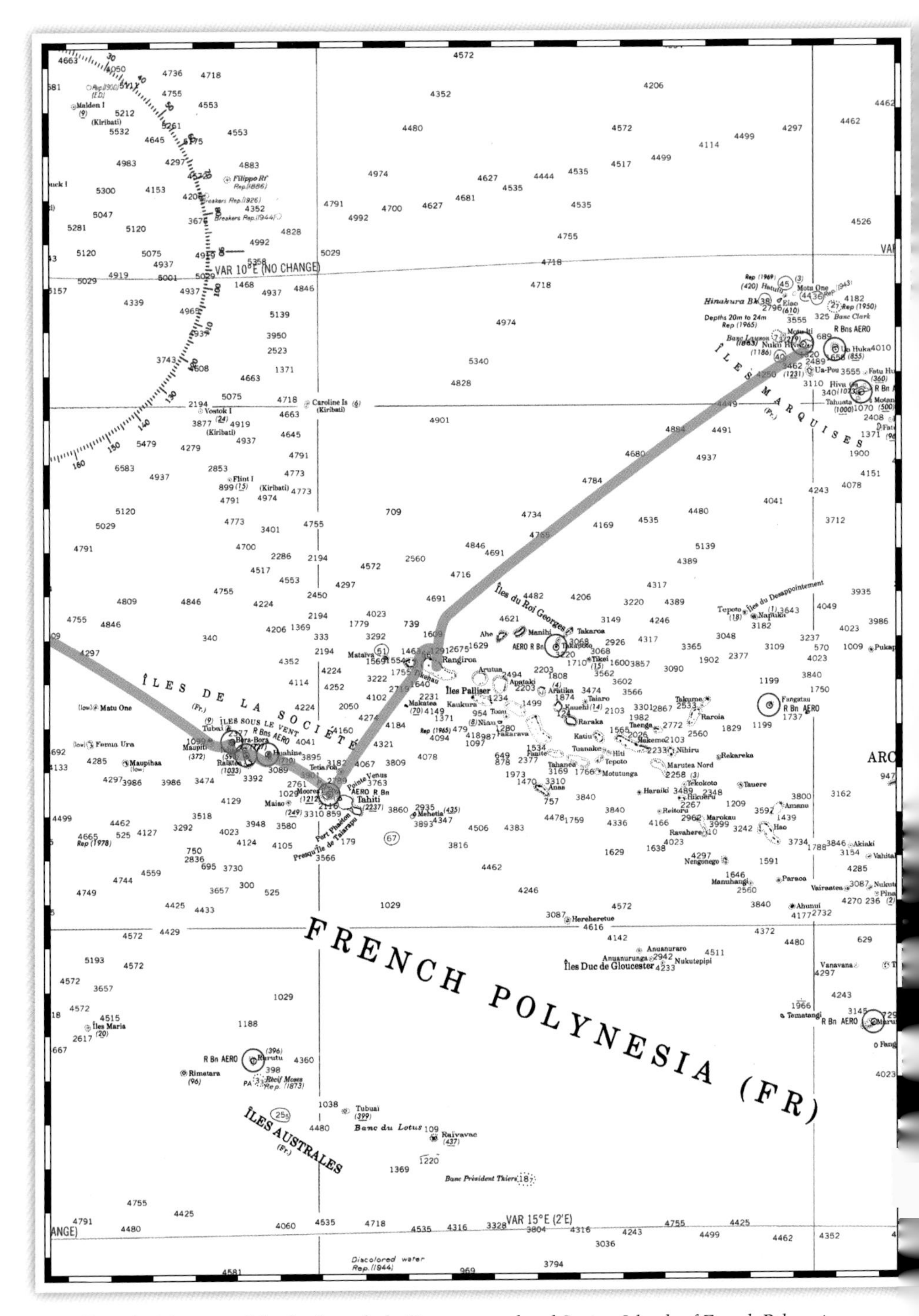

From the Marquesas Islands, through the Tuamotos and and Society Islands of French Polynesia.

I look over towards the entrance and watch as the foam from tradewind-driven seas wraps around the point, then state, "I know I am being chicken, but we could buy some insurance by having the sculling oar in place ready to go if the wind quits on us and she won't come about."

It had been more than a week since we sailed into Daniel's Bay. We'd become tired of the constant heave of the southerly ocean swell rolling into Taihoe Bay, tired of being anchored bow and stern just to achieve a semblance of comfort, tired of constantly adjusting the galley sail to direct a cooling breeze into the boat since she couldn't swing to the wind. And we'd also needed to get away from the highly enjoyable but almost constant social whirl so I could settle in and get a story off to a nagging editor while Larry went aloft and checked over the rig to ensure nothing had shifted nor chafed during the long passage from Mexico. Now we were ready to head back to Taihoe Bay, enjoy a few more days of socializing with the crews of a dozen yachts from a half dozen different countries, send off a pile of mail then do the paperwork so we could set sail for the Tuamotus.

Sailing in to Daniel's Bay had been easy: a pleasurable beat out of the wide open arms of Taihoe Bay, a four-mile downwind run with the seas directly on our stern, then a reach into protected waters. But now we had to beat out through a relatively narrow entrance right into the whitecap-crested six-foot swells. In spite of twelve years of engine-free sailing, I was apprehensive as we lifted the anchor and turned to run towards the entrance, sculling oar in place.

Just as Larry had suggested, we took two practice tacks close to the 400-foot-wide entrance, feeling the heave of the seas as they bent around the point.

Then we reached back into still waters and Larry said, "Ready to give it a go?"

I quietly gave a thumbs-up, remembering a motto we'd agreed on soon after we'd begun sailing together: share the credit, share the blame.

Larry urged *Taleisin* as close to the wind as she could go, I adjusted the jib sheet, drawing it ever tighter as the boat gathered way. As we'd expected, the wind dropped to a zephyr just as we were within a 100 feet of the sheer wall of cliff, just as we felt the swell wrapping into the bay. But Larry didn't move the tiller, letting the boat glide another 75 feet before pushing it hard alee. I had the sheet ready to fly but waited, watching for Larry's signal and aware that I just might have to reach for the sculling oar which was just behind me held in its ready-to-go position by a simple-to-release loop of line.

"Let that jib back just a bit," Larry said quietly as he pushed the tiller hard over. "Then as soon as you feel her head coming off, let it fly and sheet in as fast as you can. Don't want to lose any ground to leeward."

Now *Taleisin* began to gather way as we moved out of the wind shadow and into the full force of the 20-knot tradewinds. She heeled sharply then surged forward as she met the full force of the oncoming seas. I tried to ignore the wave battered rocks lying less than 100 feet to leeward. But now, as we'd noticed when we rowed out earlier, the wind, bent by the point of land to windward, began to give us a break. Larry followed the lift until our bowsprit pointed towards open water. One more tack and we were into clear water, well away from the cliffs.

I let out a loud peel of laughter and turned to Larry. "That sure got my blood pumping."

"That was a challenging one," Larry agreed as he turned to set the windvane. "I still get a kick out of doing it. Do we have time for some lunch before we get to Taihoe?"

People have often told us we were crazy to sail without an engine. This had not been our intention when we were building *Seraffyn*. In fact we'd been careful to build her so we could install a small diesel engine. But a year before she was ready to be launched, a friend came back from spending a year cruising around Mexico. "Can't believe how much fun I had on less than 2500 dollars," Ken told us. That figure, which in 2016 dollars would probably equate to about $12,000 US, stuck in both of our minds. Then we began pricing engines, fuel tanks – and discovered that even with the best possible discounts the cost equaled a year in Mexico or the equivalent of our entire cruising kitty.

"Why don't we sail off just like she is?" Larry suggested. "Do without an engine for five or six months – then we can come back, go to work and put one in."

I was eager to start the adventure we'd been working towards and I trusted Larry's sailing ability even though, or maybe because, I was a relative novice. After all, he had raced his engineless 28-foot Tumlaren sloop all around the waters of British Columbia before becoming a charter yacht skipper. I'd worked alongside him and been out sailing with him on several boats and knew him to be highly practical and quite risk adverse. So I agreed. This decision worked wonderfully for us, letting us head south towards Mexico just three months after launching *Seraffyn*. Within a few weeks I knew we'd never put an engine in that boat. We were having too

There was only one stretch of sandy beach in Taihoe Bay, Nuka Hiva. This where the local folks held races at low tide.

much fun to stop cruising. Besides, I liked the connection to sailors of old as we were forced to scour the pilot charts for the currents and back eddies, the wind patterns that would give us the best chance of good passages. Then there was knowing we could never be bound by schedules. I became comfortable with heaving to off a port for a half night or more until daylight arrived or tides changed or winds filled in. I also savored the space and cleanliness, the easy maintenance because our engine-free choice resulted in us having only the simplest of systems on board. But most of all, I'd come to love the team-working skills we were forced to build together. Crazy we might be, but as a 17th century poet once wrote, "There is pleasure in madness, which none but madmen know." As the years passed and our lives fell into the rhythm of exploring under sail for eight or nine months, then searching out three or four months' work, I began to realize depending only on our sails, anchors and growing skills actually kept us enjoying our peripatetic life, adding a constant challenge – both physical and mental. A touch of adventure to almost every sailing day. Larry called it "cheap thrills."

Interestingly, when we set off on *Taleisin* we began to meet a few others who understood this same madness. But even more interesting were the boats they chose: all heavy displacement, long-keeled boats with large rudders, substantial bowsprits and very large sail plans. Tim and Pauline Carr on their 28-foot, 100-year-old Falmouth working boat which took them twice around the world, Bill Sellers with his 34-foot Atkins-designed Nimbus which served not only as a long term world girdling pleasure machine but as his scrimshaw and art studio. We each admitted to our own brand of madness. And our own immeasurable joy.

We also agreed the voyage that concerned us most was the one that now faced Larry and me, through the Tuamotu Archipelago and among the steep-to coral reef-fringed volcanic islands of Polynesia.

From the moment we left Taihoe Bay and the cloud-piercing rock spires of the Marquesas Islands in our wake, I began reading everything I had on board about the islands that lay between us and Tahiti. What I read got me worrying. The Tuamotus, a chain of 80 coral atolls that now stretched across our path, is aptly named The Dangerous Archipelago. Currents among the reefs and atolls are strong and irregular; the atolls are hard to spot because many lie just below the surface of the sea, and the tallest thing on the flat sandy coral islands – or motus, as they are called – are the tops of palm trees. This meant our navigation, done with a sextant and chronometer, had to be spot on. It also meant that once we spotted our destination we had to be extra careful in our approach because these atolls rise sheer-sided from the ocean depths and would offer absolutely no

A volcanic plug marks each side at the entrance to Taihoe Bay. Though the bay offers protection from the prevailing winds, the southerly swell makes it imperative to lay to a stern anchor.

chance of anchoring if we got too close to the hull-ripping surf-pounded coral. Then there was figuring out how to time our approach to the narrow passes that lay ahead, as the pilot book mentioned tidal currents running at up to seven or eight knots out of the atolls.

Larry is the more pragmatic member of our partnership. "Put the books away. Stop worrying," he said as he handed me a handful of fresh coconut meat from a nut he'd cracked using the winch as a chopping board, the handle as a hammer. "Sailing ships have been trading among these islands for 400 years. We'll make sure we don't approach anywhere near Rangiroa until we are sure of our position. In fact, we can heave to the night before our landfall and get both an evening and a morning round of star sights to fix our position almost exactly before we make our final approach. Be good to practice some star sights the next few nights; I'm a bit rusty. Until then, come help me drop the lapper, there's a squall coming up on us."

The short-lived squall passed, and we were sailing fine again. We spent the last bits of daylight pouring over the 249 star navigation tables together to pre-compute the positions of a half dozen stars which we hoped would be visible just at nautical twilight, the time when the sun is about twelve degrees below the horizon and the stars are clearly visible but there is still enough of a horizon so Larry could measure the exact angle of each star. (I never became good at this, sticking to sun sights for over 45 years of

The entrance to Daniel's Bay lies just astern of us.

voyaging.)

I usually love that first night watch at sea, a time when I can slow down and sort through my memories of the place we've left astern and begin catching up on letter writing. As usual, our first day at sea had been tiring, full of getting ready to set sail, then storing away gear, cleaning off shore dirt, plus the addition of this star sighting practice. So I was delighted when, as soon as Larry climbed into the bunk, the skies cleared, the wind steadied and I was able to trim the sails so we ran at a steady seven knots, wing and wing under full mainsail with the lapper held out by the spinnaker pole. I loosened off the screw we used to engage the windvane clutch and adjusted the vane about ten degrees to keep a bit high on the course we'd set, then tightened the screw again. I went below and settled in at the galley table to begin answering the first of a pile of letters. Each fifteen minutes I headed out on deck, checked the horizon, the compass, and then popped back into the cabin.

Two hours and nine answered letters into my watch, I once again climbed the companionway ladder. I was barely halfway out into the cockpit when a flash of lightening lit the sky astern of us. The boom of thunder rolled over *Taleisin* in little more than the time it took me to drop back onto the cabin sole and grab my foul weather jacket from the locker next to the companionway. I stuffed one arm into the jacket and began clambering out into the cockpit. Already the wind had increased until *Taleisin* roared down the face of the growing waves. Rain began slashing at my naked legs. I reached over to release the jib sheet when all hell broke loose. *Taleisin* seemed to spin into the face of the seas, and heeled over until water began sloshing into the cockpit. The jib, with no pressure on the sheet, began to flog and crack wildly; the 20-foot spinnaker pole began to pound against the forestay. Larry rushed on deck, groggy, naked.

"Grab the tiller, head her downwind!" I yelled as I rushed forward and uncleated both the mainsail halyard and the jib halyard.

The jib slid halfway down the headstay, still making a terrible racket and shaking the boat during the time it took for Larry to steer the boat back onto course, then steadying out at its half-hoisted position which put pressure on the pole and stopped the horrid pounding. Still *Taleisin* rushed on, clearly over-canvased but gradually coming under control as I used the tack reefing lines to haul down the mainsail into the lazy jacks. By the time I had the sail down, the squall had passed by and winds dropped off to a sedate ten knots. The jib hung halfway down the headstay. The spinnaker pole appeared to be jammed against the headstay. The mainsail flopped down around the boom between the lazy jack lines.

I looked around at the mess and replied to what I felt sure was Larry's unanswered question. "I had been keeping a lookout, only was below about fifteen minutes, squall came up really fast and caught me completely unawares. I'll sort things out. You go below and dry off, climb back into the bunk. I'll give you an extra hour to sleep."

"That's not what's bothering me," Larry replied. "I was wondering why you didn't clutch in the windvane before you let go of the jib."

"The vane was clutched. It was steering just fine until that squall hit," I told him as he climbed back into the bunk.

I spent the next hour resetting the mainsail to steady us out while I sorted and reset the jib and checked for any damage. The jib sheet had wrapped itself around the end of the pole. To get the jib fully down and the pole back into position so I could rehoist the jib and get it set wing and wing once again was a lot of work. I know it would have been easier if I'd asked Larry to help but I felt the extra work was a bit of penance for not keeping a better watch, and a chance to think through what had gone wrong.

Larry obviously spent most of his next watch also thinking things through. When he called me for my next watch he said, "Come out on deck for a few minutes." He unclutched the windvane then turned to me. "Tighten this up while I watch."

I did as he asked. He then unscrewed the clutch.

"Just as I thought," Larry said. "Your little fingers just aren't getting enough pressure on that screw. You didn't get it tight enough to hold the clutch when the extra pressure of all that wind hit. So stop beating yourself up. Wasn't really your fault. Soon as we get in and anchor somewhere I'm going to fix it so this can't happen again. Now give me a hug, then go down and get some sleep."

True to his word, a day after we anchored inside the atoll of Rangiroa near the Kia Ora Hotel just next to Tiputa Pass, Larry dug out some bits of bronze and some screws and set to work at the vise on the lazarette workbench. By day's end, he had created a permanent wrench that let me put as much pressure on the windvane clutch screw as he could using his bare hands.

As he was working he said, "Been thinking about it. We need something to ensure we don't get so caught up in a book or accidentally fall asleep and miss looking around every few minutes. It's not just squalls we have to worry about – it's ships too. As soon as we get to Tahiti we need to find a countdown-type stopwatch that buzzes and flashes every eleven minutes. I timed a ship we passed on my watch. From the time it was alongside until it went below the horizon was twelve minutes. That's why I think we should set it at eleven minutes."

One more item added to the shopping list, I helped clean up and we climbed into the dinghy to snorkel along the fish-studded coral wall that lay just 200 meters from our boat. We lingered at Rangiroa for three weeks. At first it was because a half dozen cruising friends we'd met in Mexico meandered into the atoll to stop for a few days, share meals and skin diving excursions. Another week went by because Larry complained of an ear ache. Then he developed a fever. I spoke to the health official ashore, a trained nurse from France who was on a one-year contract since the islands had an acute shortage of medical personnel. I showed him the antibiotics we carried. I followed his recommendation, to have Larry take two amoxicillin tablets each day, and after a week Larry seemed to have recovered. So we headed ashore for lunch at the local resort hotel which was almost devoid of guests.

Pierre Morel, the French waiter/host, brought a drink over and sat down with us.

"Sure wish I'd had some time off this morning to get down to the supply ship," he said. "Heard the captain was selling some real fruit – crisp apples, crunchy pears. I am so tired of soft tropical stuff."

"I can run down to the quay and get you some," I offered.

"Too late. He has already started to leave. Has to get over to Tiputa Village and offload in time to leave the atoll when the tide isn't running too fast. Really tight schedule."

Larry didn't hesitate. "Fresh apples – that is what I need. It's been months since I bit into a fresh apple. Come on, Lin, forget lunch. Let's head out to the boat, grab some money, put the outboard on the dinghy and catch up with the ship."

We'd been carrying the little 2.5 horsepower outboard since a friend brought it along to Baja California. We asked for it because we'd looked over the charts and seen that most of the safest anchorages in Polynesia were often several miles from the best skin-diving spots. And Larry was eager to explore the reefs and coral walls that lay along our paths but knew the often fresh tradewinds would make it difficult to row or sail the dinghy to spots where we preferred to anchor *Taleisin*. So we'd stitched together a padded oil-proof bag on to secure on *Taleisin*'s cabin top. We'd tried the motor out a few times in Baja but it had been sitting unused for almost four months. I was pleasantly surprised when it started on the second pull and let us charge off along the chain of islands at Cheeky's top hull speed of 4.5 knots. Forty-five minutes later we were next to the ship. I yelled until

I caught the attention of one of the crew on the 200-foot ship.

"You are too late," he yelled down to me. "We're already securing the hatches."

He obviously could tell I desperately wanted the treasure that lay hidden in his hold. A few minutes later he appeared again to yell, "Okay, I spoke with the captain. He has some private stores he'll sell you. How much money you got?"

I had the equivalent to $40 US.

"I'll spend all of this," I told him, thinking of how I'd share the excess fruit with Pierre and the crews of two other cruising yachts that were anchored near us. He sent down a bucket on a line. I put my money in and we backed slightly away from the ship and waited. Ten minutes later the crew was throwing off the lines holding the ship to the pier.

The Captain himself appeared on the ship's stern and lowered the bucket to us. "These are the last of my personal stores. Enjoy."

I grabbed the small bag out of the bucket and found six crisp, cold pears, six perfect apples and not one cent of change. The ship was already steaming off before I could protest.

"Give me one of those apples," Larry said as he noticed the shocked look on my face. He took one bite and said, "Might be the most expensive apple you ever bought but tastes wonderful."

Later that evening, I learned I'd purchased a real bargain. We headed in to have a drink with Pierre and, remembering his hunger for a fresh piece of northern fruit, took along one precious apple and one very expensive pear.

Pierre's reaction was amazing.

"You are wonderful. You can never get these out here; you sometimes find them in the Tahiti shops but those are weeks old. That ship has just arrived from New Zealand so these apples are really fresh. For this I will make you a real feast and we'll open a bottle of champagne too."

Thus we had our very first taste of New Zealand grown Royal Gala apples. I have loved them over all other apples ever since. And the pears were great too.

After lingering in the lagoon for another week, Larry's ear pains returned. He agreed when I suggested we forgo exploring another Tuamotu atoll and head straight for the more sophisticated medical facilities of Papeete on Tahiti. We began preparing to leave the next day, securing all the floorboards and locker doors, and double-lashing the dinghy in its chocks on the cabin top. I was extra diligent as many of our afternoon strolls ashore had found us lingering and watching the acrobatics of dolphins that surfed and played in the six-foot standing waves which often formed in Tiputa Pass during the outgoing tide. The 20- to 25-knot tradewinds had been blowing for the past several weeks, sending waves crashing over the reefs to fill the lagoon. Though some of this huge volume of water flows back across the reefs into the sea, the majority returns via deep passes in the reef. As Rangiroa has only two passes leading out to sea and both of these are on the windward side of the lagoon, the outgoing tide is far stronger than the incoming tides. And when this outflow of water meets the tradewind-driven seas, strong overfalls occur. We wanted some outgoing current to assist us through the pass but knew there was a strong chance of burying our bow into one or more of these overfalls, and I wanted to be as prepared as possible. Fortunately Pierre had introduced us to one of the local fishermen. He told us the simple secret of timing our exit through the passes of atolls anywhere in the world. His formula: "Moon directly overhead, moon directly below your feet, wait one hour then head to sea and fish for six hours."

Soon after daylight, we reached along the inside of the atoll towards Avatura pass which is wider than Tiputa Pass.

"Looks like we shouldn't have to tack, just close reach out," Larry called down to me as I dogged the forehatch as tightly as I could.

"I'll bring out the foulies as soon as I get the skylight secured," I called back.

"Come on, Lin, we're not going to take that much water on board. Too hot and sticky for foul weather gear. If you are worried about getting a bit wet, how about doing it nude? No one's watching."

I consulted the almanac one last time to check the position of the moon. One hour ago it would have been directly on the far side of the earth. Our timing was spot-on. I climbed on deck just as the sandy motu fell away to expose the deep ocean blue of the pass. The speed at which we approached the open sea showed the tidal current had us in its grip. I began winching in the jib and my heart seemed to speed up as wave after wave reared directly in our path, humping over the river-like flow of the outgoing tide. Sheets eased just ten degrees, *Taleisin* heeled and charged through the water. She rose to the first sea, and then seemed to plunge at a steep angle into the trough behind it. Just as she as she started to rise towards the next standing sea her bowsprit speared through the crest. A foot-deep wall of water rushed the length of the foredeck, hit the hatch coamings and sent a shower of spray five feet into the air then back towards the cockpit to coat both of us in glistening droplets of saltwater. I couldn't decide whether to jump up out of the way of the oncoming torrent or to stay right where I was in case Larry needed me to adjust the jib sheet or ease out the mainsail. Before I could make a decision, *Taleisin* headed downhill again on the back of the sea and shed all the water from her deck. She rose more gracefully to the next overfall.

Above the hiss of *Taleisin* rushing through the water, and the roar of surf pounding on the reef that was now falling away in our wake, I heard Larry shout, "Ease the sheets – we're clear."

I let the jib sheet slip through my hand as Larry brought *Taleisin* onto a beam reach. Then I jumped up to hug his damp body, a hug he returned with gusto. As *Taleisin* settled onto my favorite point of sail and my heart beat returned to normal, I headed below for a towel.

"I know it's a bit early but while you're down there, how about getting us a drink?" Larry suggested.

I climbed back into the cockpit with two small shots of rum.

"Here's to cheap thrills," Larry said as he poured a small libation overboard then settled in to savor the rest.

Monica's family has run one of Taihoe Bay's small grocery stores for three generations. She flirted outrageously with Larry. He returned the favor.She always sent him home with fresh fruit as a gift for me.

The Bastille Day celebrations at Papeete bring together the best dance teams from throughout French Polynesia.

Chapter 6

A Chance Encounter

We'd been at anchor in Apia, Samoa for almost a week. The time had rushed by as we obtained visas for New Zealand and answered the last of the mail we'd received in Pago Pago. With all necessary paperwork completed, we enjoyed spending the rest of each day with a steady round of shared meals and shore excursions, as cruising sailors we had met along our route sailed in to anchor nearby. On this day, we'd decided on a quiet evening by ourselves and after dinner on board rowed ashore for a walk. For some reason, instead of heading towards the promenade fronting the town, we turned towards the commercial port.

A half dozen local fishing boats and one ship lay secured along the quay. The ship was a down-at-heels freighter with a Panamanian flag hanging limply over its stern. Its captain lounged on the side deck.

"Where's this ship headed?" I called up to him.

"Taiwan. It's on its last voyage, going to the wreckers there," he answered in a smooth-sounding British accent.

"Have any charts you don't need?" I couldn't resist asking.

"Whole world is in the chart room. Come on up and take what you want.

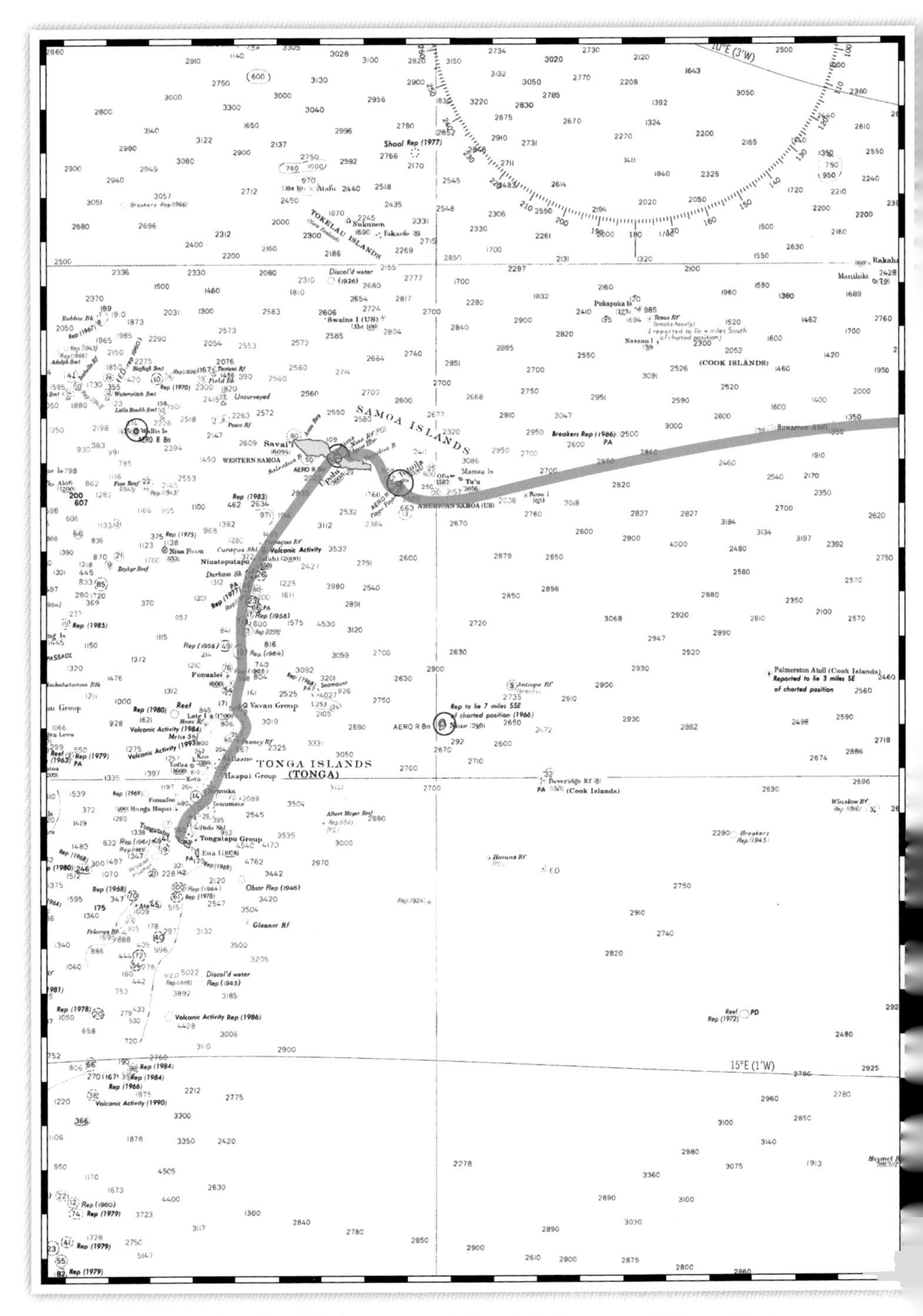

Our route from French Polynesia onward through the Samoan and Tongan Islands.

Only need to keep the ones from here north," replied the ship's captain.

For the next hour we learned about the life of a captain on a tramp steamer, chatted about the far-flung communities this ship had serviced.

"Last freight she carried we dropped off a few days ago at a really isolated island just 200 miles from here," Graeme told us. "First ship to get inside their lagoon. Last month the Australian Navy gave the islanders a gift; they blasted a pass through the reef. Up till then we had to heave to outside the reef and islanders came out with small boats. Dropped barrels of diesel overboard and they towed them in through a small boat passage. Always carried lots of ice cream bars for the kids. Got some spares – want one?"

As we clambered down the ship's ramp, loaded with almost 100 charts to take us to destinations beyond New Zealand, Graeme said, "I'll bring along a sketch of the entrance to Niuatoputapu when the mate and I come over to your boat for lunch tomorrow. Friendly folks there would probably love having some yachts come by. Want to look up in my log and be sure I give you the correct entry bearings."

This chance encounter led to the kind of adventure I think every potential voyager dreams of, one I'd worried we'd never find along the heavily cruised tradewind route: a chance to experience and gain an intimate understanding of a different culture.

Though we could have tied up at the town quay and used a boarding plank to land, we chose to secure Taleisin a few blocks away where we felt comfortable diving overboard for a swim, even though this meant using the dinghy to reach shore.

Three days later after we turned southward to head through the pass between Savai'i and Upulo, the two main islands of Samoa, and make for Niuatoputapu, Larry and I reminisced about our voyage through French Polynesia. The day after we had arrived in Papeete Larry had gone to the medical clinic where the doctor had the answer to his constant round of ear infections and fevers.

"Common problem among folks who are new to the tropics and love skin diving," he told Larry. "We call it diver's ear. Better to prevent it than have to cure it. So from now on, every time you plan to go in the water put a small drop of olive oil in each ear. Then mix up a solution of 20 percent vinegar, 80 percent isopropyl alcohol and put a drop in each ear when you get out of the water for the day and be sure it sits for four or five minutes. But right now here are the drops you need to clear up the bacteria that's causing the problem. Take a week or two off the diving and you'll be fine. "

From then on we'd been in the water almost every day and found the skin diving on the coral reefs fringing most of the islands provided endless hours or amusement – and lots of good eating.

The sailing between Tahiti and Samoa had been relatively easy, the anchorages varied and interesting. But as we began talking about the interpersonal relationships we'd had, we both realized we'd hardly gotten to know any of the local Polynesian people because our days had been filled with an ever-changing kaleidoscope of cruising sailors from a dozen different countries. Meeting these folks was easy because they were usually anchored only a few hundred yards away and we had so much in common that it was easy to start a conversation. This led to a merry-go-round of shared meals, joint excursions. Some fellow cruisers became just a pleasant memory, a name in our guest log; others had become close friends and meandered through the islands with us almost like a moveable yachting club. But any knowledge of local life and politics we gained had come through three people we'd met only because they too were living on board and only one of them was actually Polynesian.

One of those was Bernard Moitessier. Within hours of anchoring two blocks away from the center of Papeete we found ourselves on board *Tamata*, the 31-foot steel boat he now called home. Bernard, born and raised in Vietnam, held a French passport, thus could reside in French Polynesia without the need for a visa. During his two circumnavigations, Bernard had previously spent several years in these islands, including two on the atoll of Ahe where he tried to grow fruit and vegetables and convince the local people to adopt what he felt would be more successful cultivation methods. Now, after finding he could not afford to live comfortably in the

That's five gallons of kerosene in the tank on my bike rack.
The bikes made shopping easier, and more fun too.

One of the winners of the Papeete dance competition. I came to wonder how the judges could differentiate between the amazing dancers and dance groups who performed for us.

US or France, he had sailed away from what he called "the madness of civilization," looking for a peaceful place to write a book on the practical aspects of voyaging to complement his highly successful sailing narratives.[1] For the past year he had been secured at the quay right in the center of Papeete and spent much of his time lobbying against the over-development of the waterfront and protesting against the testing of nuclear weapons at Mururoa, one of the southernmost Tuamotu atolls. Though we had met on several other occasions, this was the first time we spent more than a

1 His books, *The Long Way* and *Cape Horn, the Logical Route*, were bestsellers on both sides of the Atlantic. In an altruistic gesture, Bernard gave the proceeds away to the Catholic Church. Though he never completed the manuscript he was writing in Papeete, the book was published posthumously under the title, *A Sea Vagabond's World*.

few hours together. We both found his company enjoyable, but for very different reasons.

Larry loved the logic and utter simplicity of Bernard's latest boat. Bernard had always preferred steel hulls but wanted to avoid the problems he'd had with *Joshua*, his previous boat. She had developed serious corrosion problems which started behind the interior woodwork and under much of the woodwork on deck. Thus *Tamata* had been built so that every piece of joinery could be easily unbolted and removed to allow him to inspect and repaint the complete interior of the hull. On deck he had no wood other than gratings that were held in place with easy-to-remove bolts. Among many other items that caught Larry's eye was the diesel engine installation. Instead of being hidden behind elaborate joinery which would have made the boat seem far smaller, it was out in the open and served as the companionway ladder with a simple padded one-piece cover with sewn-on foot prints marking where each step should be.

"When I want to use the engine, I simply take the cover off," Bernard explained. "Yes, that means it is noisy. But I only use it for a short time to get in and out of a port; I am in the cockpit anyway so noise doesn't matter. And because it is so easy to get to, it is easy to service and keep clean."

To me, Bernard was the charmer, the pied piper. We spent several mid-day hours in the cool of *Taleisin*'s cabin talking of his view of local life and politics then going over his book project together. Soon his tribe of young followers came to know if he wasn't on board *Tamata* when they got out of school each afternoon, he probably was on board *Taleisin*. As soon as he heard their chatter and giggles, Bernard would excuse himself and, trailed by a gaggle of laughing youngsters, head off to lead them for a scavenge along the local reef or a game of football in the park just across the road from where *Taleisin* was moored.

The second person who gave us an interesting insight into local life was Dorine Samuelson. She and her family lived on the Sparkman and Stevens 37-footer, *Swan II*, which was moored just a few boats down from *Tamata*. We met two days after we arrived in Papeete. Larry and I had been to the post office where we'd picked up a package containing three months' worth of mail. As was our custom whenever we received a large bunch of mail, we found a café, ordered cool drinks and a bowl of gelato, then settled in to open and linger over each letter. Within a few minutes we'd discovered four unexpected checks for articles we'd sent off from Mexico.

"Come on, let's celebrate. I'll order another bowl of gelato for each of us," Larry said.

The young girl seated at the next table eyed us closely. "I am never allowed to have two bowls of gelato," she said.

Soon we were seated with four-year-old Nicki Samuelson and her parents. They had spent a year sailing *Swan II* from Los Angeles and now her mother, Dorine, a French national, was working as a nurse in Papeete while her father, David, upgraded their boat. Soon Larry had promised to rig *Cheeky,* our eight-foot tender, and take Nicki sailing.

Most afternoons thereafter, as Nicki and Larry skimmed about the harbor under the bright orange and yellow sail, Dorine and I shared afternoon tea on board *Swan II* or *Taleisin*. She was enjoying their planned year-long stay in Papeete, but one of her big concerns was the two-tier pay system that left her feeling uncomfortable and sometimes resented by locals. In order to entice skilled workers from France to spend a year or two in French Polynesia, the government paid the French nationals working in French Polynesia bonuses which, with the addition of free housing, equaled more than three times the salary paid to Tahitians.

"The French government is offering scholarships to promising local students," Dorine made clear. "But many of the youngsters get terribly homesick and come back before they get their degrees. It's going to take years and years before this system can end."

One exceptionally fun afternoon with Dorine was spent giving my wardrobe a much needed upgrade. I hate shopping, unless it is for boat gear or food. But sometimes it's a necessary evil.

As I have found throughout my sailing career, I tend to gain weight when we live on shore for more than a short period. As soon as we set off on an ocean passage, the weight peels away. Since leaving Mexico, I had lost the 20 pounds I'd gained while building *Taleisin*. Few of my going-ashore clothes now fit. Dorine knew all the local shops and enjoyed visiting them. So, encouraged by Larry and fueled by the unexpected checks we'd received, I set off to find some new clothes.

Along with some beautiful pareaus, jeans and tops, I also indulged, with Dorine's encouragement, in eight pairs of lacy French knickers – which cost far more than I had ever considered paying for any undergarment. When I modeled my new clothes for Larry later that evening, I purposefully didn't mention the cost of those knickers; I just delighted in his appreciation. Three months later, when we arrived at the Tongan island of Vava'u, a local named Alofi rowed up to *Taleisin* and offered to take care of my very large bag of laundry for a fair price. The laundry was delivered back to me at the time specified, neatly folded into the sailbag I'd provided. As I stored everything away I found two of Larry's shirts, two of my tops and all of my French knickers missing. I was furious. When I mentioned this

These stunning volcanic peaks mark the head of Pao Pao Bay, which is also known as Cooks Bay on Mo'orea.

to some of the other cruising sailors at the local café that evening, the café owner and all in attendance told us Alofi had ripped off so many people that there was a warning against him in the *Moon Travel Guide*. They all urged me to speak to the local police. Larry insisted we do it immediately and Robyn Coleman, the café owner escorted us to the police station.

"We have had many complaints against this man," the police officer said. "But we cannot press charges unless the items stolen are worth at least $150 US."

Now I was in a quandary: should I let Larry know how much I had paid/wasted on underpants, or should I let a scoundrel continue his nefarious ways?

I hesitated, then after a few minutes reluctantly admitted to the price of my Papeete shopping spree.

Amelia and Charles Maulaz lived on board their boat for several years here in Pao Pao Bay. Evenings with these two was always filled with laughter and interesting insights into local life.

"$150 US? You paid that amount *just for the knickers?*" Larry's jaw dropped.

But the case went ahead. Alofi was brought in to the station. The police confronted him and asked us to be there to confirm the list of missing items. Alofi looked contrite as he admitted he could get some of the items back to me, but not all of the knickers as those had gone to his girlfriend who refused to return them. He was sentenced to 100 hours of community service.

The evening sailors' radio net carried the whole story, headlined by *Lin Pardey lost her Knickers*. Almost three years later, I was being reminded of those overpriced bits of French lace by sailors we met far beyond the waters of Tonga.

Three weeks meandered past before we set sail to cross the sixteen miles that separated the hustle and bustle of Tahiti and the stunning beauty and village atmosphere of Mo'orea. The morning after we anchored in Cook's Bay, I was startled by the laughter-filled voice of Amelia Maulaz. She had rowed quietly alongside in a dugout canoe.

It was only as she began depositing fresh fruit into *Taleisin*'s cockpit that she called out, "Welcome to my home."

I admired the way this big handsome woman managed to climb gracefully out of a relatively unstable canoe and onto *Taleisin*, all the while controlling her windblown pareau so it not only avoided catching on our lifelines but also kept her modesty intact.

Amelia was a Pitcairn Islander – and the third person we came to spend time with in French Polynesia who shared local insights and stories. A direct ancestor of one of the Tahitians who had settled on that exceptionally isolated island along with Fletcher Christian and his crew from the Royal Navy vessel HMS *Bounty*. Raised and schooled among a population of fewer than 70 people, Amelia found further education options limited. So when she wanted to go to college, she had been sent to live with an aunt in Papeete. She fell in love with Charles, a French sailor and structural engineer. Together they sailed back to Pitcairn on board their 45-foot steel ketch so Amelia could visit her family – her first visit in many years. But it was only a short visit as there was no safe place to leave their boat, even for a full day on shore together. So they had anchored here in Cook's Bay and raised their two children on board.

Laughter punctuated most of Amelia's sentences, even the most serious discussions we had when her husband Charles joined the conversations. Our exchanges were lightened by her good-natured humor. It was from Amelia that I first got a sense of the Polynesian concept of extended family and community responsibility that left no child an orphan, and no one consigned to an old age home.

"Do you ever miss your mother?" I asked one day.

"Which one?" she said in a surprised voice. "I am Polynesian. I have lots of mothers, the one I was born to, the aunt on Pitcairn Island who cared for me when my mother was ill, the aunt here in Tahiti who I lived with while I went to school, the auntie here in Mo'orea who helped me when I was first pregnant and Charles had to be away for several months."

Charles laughed as he described the results of this situation. "It is much better in many ways than our European insular families, but sometimes it can be overwhelming – like when our children were born and I couldn't get near Amelia because she was surrounded by her 'mothers' – one holding each hand, one rubbing each foot. I felt superfluous."

Both Larry and I treasured this glimpse into actual Tahitian life, even as we realized it was only that: a tiny and limited glimpse. Getting to know more about the complexities of history and politics would take more time and the ability to speak French and Tahitian if I wanted a deeper understanding. For instance, when I asked about the local reaction to Oscar Temaru's call for Tahitian independence, it quickly became obvious that the subject was one that made both Amelia and Charles uncomfortable. And with what amounted to superficial contact with actual Tahitians, we learned little about the evolving political scene, or the aspirations of the Tahitian people, either immediate or longer-term.

We recognized the distinctive sail plan of Mike Kris' Gilpie *as we approached the island of Raiatea. Together we sailed onward to Taha'a and found a quiet anchorage where we could skin dive, relax and catch up with each other. Mike headed north to Hawaii when the cyclone season approached.*

It was almost dark as we cleared the Apolima Strait and trimmed *Taleisin*'s sails to reach southward 160 miles towards Niuatoputapu.

When I set dinner out in the cockpit I commented, "If only I had taken some time to learn more than a few words of French, we could have

Rudy and Mary Kok on their Cape George 31-foot cutter Eleu *challenged us to a race out through the pass at Raiatea and on to Bora Bora. Here they are punching through the steep waves at the pass entrance. They too headed north to Hawaii after sailing through these islands and on to Samoa.*

made friends on shore." In the back of my mind was the language tapes I'd bought in preparation for our voyage to Polynesia. We'd listened to them for about a week when we sailed south towards Baja California. But once we began brushing up on our Spanish by using it each day in Baja California, the tapes had been put aside and soon forgotten. "Laziness, sheer laziness," I said.

"Ease up," Larry rejoined. "We had a good time in the islands. Met lots of interesting people. The time sure went fast. Besides, some of the Australian and New Zealand sailors we've met will be an introduction to local life in their countries when we head south for the cyclone season. And now the cruising fleet is started to split up, you'll probably have more time to meet local folks."

Larry was right; the cruising fleet was getting ever smaller, the farther west we sailed. Many of the American and Canadians we'd met along the way had decided to turn north from Tahiti and return home via Hawaii; those from the east coast were planning to truck their yachts across country from Vancouver or San Francisco. In Bora Bora several of the fleet decided to take a more northerly route towards Vanuatu or the Solomon islands. And in Samoa we had said farewell to a half dozen cruisers who, realizing they only had a few months to enjoy before the cyclone season set in, chose to head directly towards the islands of Fiji or Australia's Great Barrier Reef.

"You head down and get some sleep," I said when I heard the ship's bell ring eight times. "If this wind stays steady, we should spot the volcano north of Niuatoputapu at daylight tomorrow."

Taleisin shouldered her way across the tradewind-driven seas at a steady six-and-a-half knots, the small jib and full mainsail drawing perfectly. Stars seemed to explode across the sky as the last glow of the sun's light fell away and the islands of Samoa slowly dropped below the horizon. I sat quietly in the cockpit until I heard Larry snoring steadily in the leeward pilot berth. Then I carried our dinner dishes below and was just reaching for the dish soap when I heard wild shouting. I grabbed a flashlight as I rushed into the cockpit. As I turned to look forward, I caught the tiny glow of a cigarette being waved frantically in the air a few boat lengths ahead of our plunging bowsprit.

I reacted almost instinctively, reaching down to shove the tiller to leeward. A rough-looking open workboat manned by four fishermen slipped by less than a foot from the side of *Taleisin*. The red glare of our port running light illuminated their frightened faces. Two of the men were paddling hard to clear us; one was still standing amidships holding the lit cigarette he'd been waving to try to attract attention. The other one had obviously been trying to pull up the anchor which had been holding them over a fifteen-fathom shoal – a shallow feature that I later noticed on the chart.

My first reaction was anger – anger that they'd been out there without any lights at all. Then, slowly, this turned to anger at me for not being on deck watching. I blurted my feelings out to Larry who had been roused by the shouting, the sudden course change.

"Those guys probably couldn't afford a flashlight, or they didn't have spare batteries," Larry commented. "Speed we're moving, could have sunk their boat, hurt them. They sure were lucky you got on deck just in time."

But as he slowly drifted back to sleep I went out into the cockpit to think of how, for the second time since we'd sailed into the South Pacific, luck had been on our side: first when we came within a few yards of sailing onto a sleeping pair of whales, and now when we just missed running down four hapless fishermen who obviously hadn't expected anyone to be sailing along this route. Instead of reading a book or writing letters as I usually did once we were well clear of the land, I stayed on deck watching the waters around us all through the rest of my watch as I wondered how much more luck we could possibly have in reserve.

As the sun began lightening the horizon, the sky to the east turning from black to lavender, the perfect volcanic cone of Tafahi could be seen rising slowly from the sea ahead of us. By mid-day we'd reached past its heavily wooded steep-to side and began our approach to the reef fronting Niuatoputapu. The four-mile-long island lies along an east-west axis. With the fifteen-knot tradewinds blowing from the southeast, the seas began to flatten out as we turned to run westward about a half mile off the reef. I dropped the headsail into the jib net and lashed it down, then raised the staysail so it would be easier to maneuver through the pass when we located it.

Meanwhile, Larry was searching the shoreline with binoculars and soon called to me, "There, just to the east of the last house. Has to be the leading marks."

I had to borrow the binoculars to find the two wooden stakes he indicated, their white-painted tops just making it possible to distinguish them from the palm trees around them. As soon as the two markers began to line up, we could see the color differentiation of the water that showed where the new pass cut through the reef. But caution, encouraged by the makeshift manner of the leading markers, made both of us reluctant to turn and reach through, into the lagoon.

"Okay, let's heave to just off the pass. You take care of the boat. I'll put on my mask and fins, swim through then we'll know exactly what to expect," Larry stated.

As I watched for the spurt of his snorkel and the splash of his fins while he swam along the edges of the pass, I wondered if we were being overly cautious. But then I thought of the 7800 hours we'd spent building this boat, the hundreds of hours we'd then worked getting it ready to go cruising. The hour this caution was costing us was nothing in comparison – and our delay paid a pleasant dividend.

By the time Larry had climbed back on board, the first of two small canoes I'd seen setting off from the beach arrived at the pass, its two young paddlers shouting and beckoning us to follow them.

Larry chuckled. "They probably have no idea of how much water we need. Glad I swam through. The pass is real clear most of the way, but just before you get to where we have to turn to starboard, there is a coral head with only four or five feet of water on it that sticks out into the channel."

I eased off the staysail sheet as Larry pulled on the tiller to head towards the pass. I loved this feeling, skimming with complete confidence along a route which we now knew held no dangers as we glided into the smooth water that opened up between the enfolding arms of the reef.

Adding to special feeling of this moment were the two canoes and four laughing youngsters who came out to escort us towards the area free of coral heads, just off the scattering of houses that lay near a rough stone landing. As soon as *Taleisin* settled back against her anchor, Larry grabbed all the fenders we had and hung them over the side. The young girl in the first canoe shyly handed me two bottles of a golden-colored liquid which I later learned was a specialty of this particular island: highly condensed lemon juice. Her companion passed over a basket full of succulent smelling fruit. When the second canoe, crewed by the two teenaged boys, came alongside, the whole foursome seemed to lose their shyness and almost immediately the air was filled with a flood of English, spoken as if this was the very first time it had been used outside a schoolroom.

"Where you from? What are your names? Why are you here?"

Their laughter and enthusiasm as they discussed each answer and came back with ever more questions made it hard to resist inviting them on board. As the oldest girl climbed up, she settled gracefully onto the cockpit coaming and formally introduced herself.

"I am Molokeini but my friends just call me Keini."

Her younger compatriots were far less decorous, trying to peek inside the cabin, giggling and chattering away in Tongan.

"Come on in," I said as I climbed down the companionway.

They eagerly followed me below.

"Will you stay here for another day so I can take you home to my family?" Keini asked as soon as she was inside *Taleisin*.

Her words confirmed what I had sensed from the moment we spotted Niuatoputapu. Here was one of the true gifts of cruising: a chance to have an intimate look at another culture, another way of life. What I could never have imagined as we showed these youngsters more of our small floating home was how far-reaching this gift would turn out to be – a gift bestowed by a chance encounter on the Samoan waterfront with a tramp steamer captain.

Though very different from the less traveled paths we'd taken on Seraffyn, the so-called "Milk Run" proved to be just as memorable. Many of the cruising sailors who shared anchorages with us along the way have become life-long friends.

Never have we felt so welcome as we did in the islands of Tonga.

CHAPTER 7

THE FRIENDLY ISLES PART I

"Mrs Leen, Mrs Leen, you must go the capital today," called Taniela as he paddled towards us the next morning. "The Chief said I am to take you ashore right now!"

We recognized the teenaged boy who had come to greet us the day before. He and his friends had stayed on board long after two big bowls of popcorn had been devoured. I had noticed Taniela looking at the guitar I kept secured in the pilot berth.

"Do you play?" I had asked.

He turned instantly shy, but Keini spoke up. "He is good."

So I unlashed the guitar and, to break the ice, using four of the nine chords I knew, strummed and sang a few bars of "Grandma's Feather bed." Larry sang along with me and soon the two girls were joining the chorus. Then I handed the guitar to Taniela. He softly strummed a few chords then settled in to a gentle syncopated rhythm. The cabin became a perfect sound chamber as four young voices sang a subdued version of a Tahitian tamari, then urged us to sing along. Two hours later their songs and laughter were

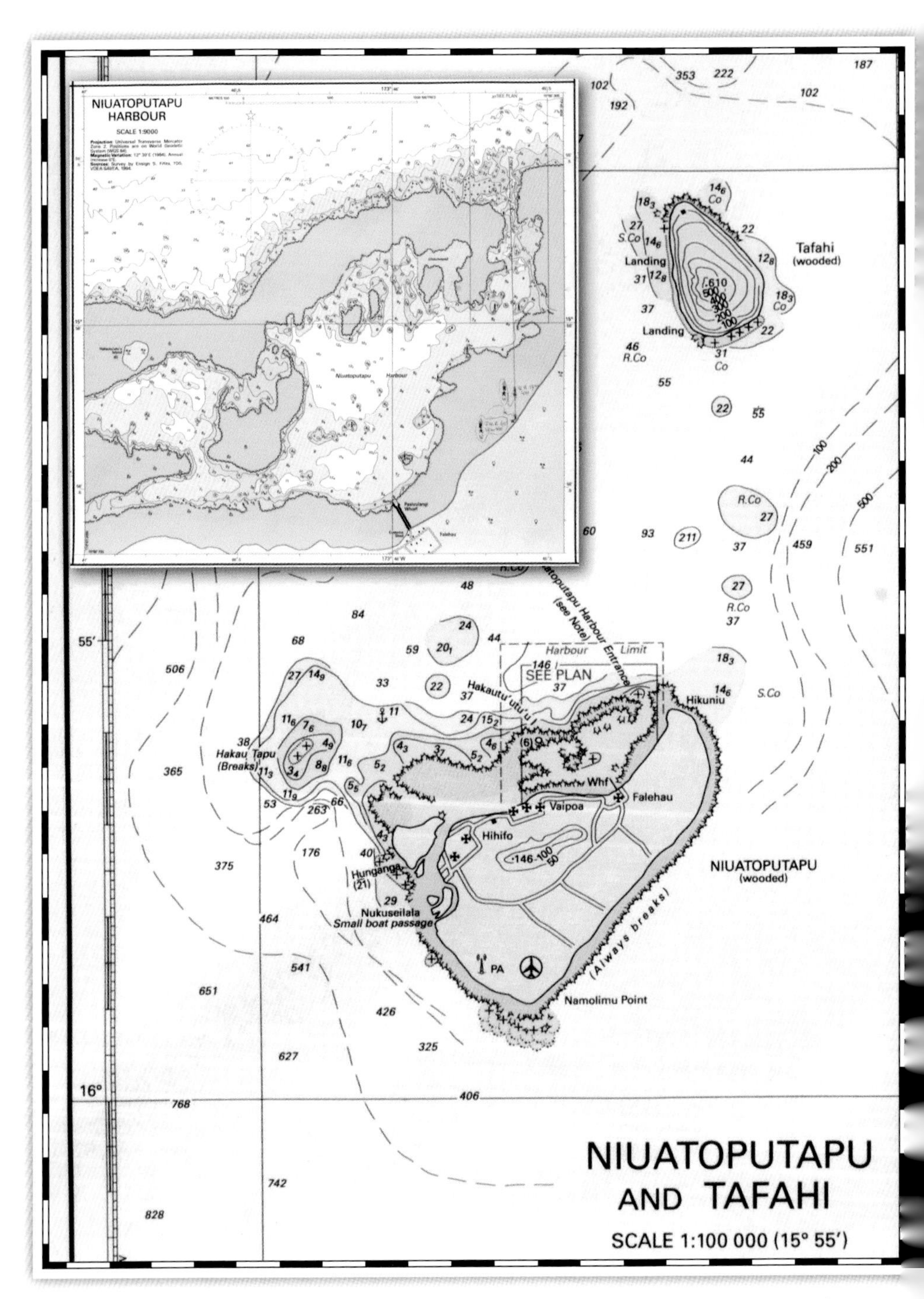

The two northern-most islands of Kingdom of Tonga. The inset shows details of the channel blasted through the reef by the Australian Navy as a gift to the people of Niuatoputapu.

At high tide the reef that protects Niuatoputapu is just awash but it still provides full protection to the anchorage. The passage between the reef and the volcanic island of Tafahi is a main thoroughfare and mating ground for humpback whales.

still ringing in my ears as they rowed ashore while Larry and I stayed in the cockpit to finish stowing our sails and put up our sun cover.

"Too late to launch the dinghy," Larry said. "Not sure how or where we are supposed to clear in here. Can't see any office near the landing wharf. Let's wait until tomorrow to explore the situation."

I agreed as I couldn't see any officials or motorized vehicles on shore. A few fishermen were pulling their boats up the beach. Three horses were grazing in front of the two dozen thatch and corrugated iron-sided homes visible from our anchorage. A church bell rang out. But otherwise the only sound we heard as we settled in the cockpit to enjoy a glass of wine together was the murmur of waves washing against the reef a half mile to windward, the flapping of the quarantine and visitors flag that hung from our starboard spreader and the snap of the Canadian flag which was secured to *Taleisin*'s lazyjacks above my head.

We were unlashing the lines that held *Cheeky* on her cabin top chocks after a refreshing night's sleep in the still waters of the lagoon when the Taniela came alongside.

Larry quietly said to me, "Remember what that Swedish official said years ago? 'Welcome to paradise but even in paradise there is a snake; I am here to collect the harbor dues.'"

"Hope this snake will be as easy to appease," I laughed. Then I went

I enjoyed taking the dinghy out to explore the rock pools surrounding the small motu on the outer reef of Niuatoputapu while Larry dove along the reef edge looking for dinner.

below and packed up our ship's papers and our passports.

Keini was waiting to help us land.

"We must go to the capital," she repeated as she took my hand and led us along the track fronting her village. Her words became almost like a chant as we walked past each gaggle of children who seemed to appear magically along the narrow sandy road.

"How far is the capital?" I asked as another half dozen children decided to skip along with us.

"It is in Hihifo, at the other end of the island," she said as we walked past a densely wooded area, then a church, a school and another small cluster of palm-leaf roofed homes. "Just two more villages to pass," Keini added as she shooed one of the smaller kids out of my path.

So onward we walked for two miles, returning greetings with the adults who shyly waved from the front yards of their homes. By the time Keini announced, "There is the capital," I felt almost like an honored international dignitary. A noisy train of youngsters, which seemed to make up a large percentage of the total population of 1200 people, surrounded us, calling importantly to each person they saw, "We are bringing them to the capital."

Ahead of us, standing just a bit away from another two dozen simple but very tidy looking wooden and thatch homes, was a more formal wooden structure – not large, but distinguished from the buildings around it by a western-style verandah, a solid-looking tin roof and a tall radio antennae attached to its side wall.

The children scattered to stand at the edge of the clearing when "The Chief" came to the edge of the verandah to greet us. We'd already guessed he was the chief as we'd seen him walk out of the building – the Capitol – carrying a pair of polished shoes. He'd sat down on the bench nearest the door, put the shoes on, stood up, brushed his dazzling white shirt into order.

Then, when we were almost at the steps leading on to the verandah, he said, "Malo e lelei," which we now knew was the Tongan word for welcome. "I am the Captain of the Port," he explained. "Also the head of customs, the postmaster, the representative of the Bank of Tonga, the head radio operator. And, the Chief of Police."

He pointed towards a tiny wooden structure with barred windows but wide-open door as he recited his last title, and added, "And that is the jailhouse."

The Chief explained we were the second yacht to anchor inside the reef. "In the past, a few sailors have anchored outside the reef where there is a small shoaling area but, as this same shoal is a favorite spot for mating whales, they didn't stay more than one night," he told us, his English accented in a way that showed he had spent time with a teacher from New Zealand. "The other yacht that came inside the reef only stayed for two nights and didn't come to the capital. So I don't really know what to do with you. Let me write down everything about you and I will radio to Nuku'alofa."

So: no snakes in this island paradise. Instead we were sent away from the capital with a bag containing two perfectly ripe mangos, a handful of lemons and some yams, plus our entourage of children which dwindled in size as we meandered our way eastward, back towards Keini's village.

Later that afternoon, after we'd cooled down by snorkeling along the inside of the reef, our original four visitors arrived with another four youngsters in tow.

"Your guitar, can we play with it? The photo album, can we show it?"

By our fourth afternoon at anchor, the afternoon guitar-playing session had grown to include a dozen youngsters. Each new one was given a carefully narrated tour of *Taleisin* by one of our first visitors who, I could sense by the serious tone of their voices, had claimed guardianship rights. Then the photo album I'd assembled with pictures of our families, the home where we'd built *Taliesin*, some photos of her under construction and others of the people and places we'd met along our way, was passed around with

There were just three motorized vehicles on the island when we first sailed in to Niaitoputapu. Now, 30 years later, there are still only a dozen.

each photo carefully explained by previous visitors.

When the sun began to set, our guests paddled off, calling, "Come ashore tomorrow and we'll take you to the swimming hole."

It was at the swimming hole that we began to know some of the island adults. A fresh water stream had worn a grotto-like pool into the volcanic rock that makes up the majority of the island. A few steps had been cut into the side of the pool to allow easy access. A large ledge of overhanging rocks protected much of the pool from the blazing sun. As I watched the older Tongan women climb into the cool sweet water and immediately make their way into the shaded area, I noticed they were far more modest than the people we'd seen in Polynesia and Samoa. All remained carefully covered in long loose dresses or pareaus, even in the water. The few older men who came down to cool off wore lava lava-like wrappings over their bathing trunks. We'd come to know the ages of our young entourage so I could calculate the approximate transition age from the immodesty of youth to the modesty of maturity at about twelve years of age. But I did these calculations *after* I'd climbed into the pool in my own bikini. Despite it being relatively modest, I soon climbed back out of the water and returned wrapped in the pareau I'd worn for the walk here. From the warmer greetings of the older women I could see I'd done the right thing. All shyness seemed to disappear as they asked one youngster or another to translate their questions and our answers – and occasionally tried to use a few English phrases themselves.

Later as we walked back towards where our dinghy sat waiting, escorted by Keini and Mele, Larry quietly said to me, "If the last few evenings and the time we just spent at the swimming hole are anything to go by, *Taleisin* won't be able to hold all the people who want to join the music time on board because I would expect some of their parents would want to come along too. Why don't you tell Keini you'll bring your guitar ashore this evening and we can all meet at the wharf when it cools down?"

Back on board *Taleisin* we settled into the forward bunk for an afternoon siesta, the breeze directed into the cabin by our wind scoop making it cool enough that I actually pulled a sheet over my bare body. Less than a chapter into the latest novel from the stash we'd picked up in the laundry trading library at Pago Pago, I heard the sound of an anchor chain rumbling out not far from us.

"Lin, you are a regular jack-in-the-box," Larry commented as I almost trampled him in my rush to pop my head out the forehatch. "Whoever it is, they aren't going anywhere immediately. Relax."

But I'd recognized *Pegasus*, a 37-foot Dutch-designed steel ketch built from a bare hull and deck by an Australian family. We'd met the Metheralls in Bora Bora and rendezvoused with them again in Apia. Jan and Peter were headed homeward after a year of cruising with their three children: Tim – now sixteen years old; Brendan, fourteen; and Bridget, the youngest at twelve. They were the only other cruisers who had been excited when we showed them the drawing we'd been given to guide us into the lagoon at Niuatoputapu. Jan played the guitar and Bridgette the ukulele. I knew they would be the perfect addition to the planned evening event.

I wrapped a pareau around myself, then climbed into *Cheeky* and rowed over to tell them of our plans.

"I'll make up a bag of popcorn to take along," Jan said. "Need to use it up because I read that we can't take any un-popped corn into New Zealand. And I have loads on board."

When we all rowed ashore a few hours later, no one was there to greet us. I felt just a bit concerned that our invitation hadn't been understood. But I need not have worried. Soon Keini and Taniela came running down the lane leading to the landing.

"Mele has gone to tell the teacher you really have brought your guitar along. He said he would bring his too."

The two shopping bags full of popcorn disappeared within minutes and the evening sing-along slowly grew as more people wandered down

The fine mats woven here are treasured throughout the other islands of Tonga.

to join us. Three more guitars arrived, none with a full complement of strings. But even with one or two strings missing, the guitars added to the swelling mood, and the music filled the tropical evening air. Soon the blond heads of the three young Metheralls were almost lost among the curly long black tresses of local children.

As all of us rowed away from shore, Tim announced; "The school teacher said he is setting up a games day tomorrow afternoon. Asked us kids to be on the local team, asked everyone to come along too and to bring more popcorn."

Between Jan and me, we produced three garbage bags full of pop-corn for what turned out to be island-wide soccer and volley-ball game event. Though at first it was kids who excitedly grabbed handfuls of popcorn, slowly their parents came along and tried a single piece, then lost their inhibitions and grabbed handfuls too.

By the time ten days had passed I'd come to realize how simply but well these people lived, how easily they welcomed visitors into their lives. I'd spent some of my time in the cool of the open-sided working shed with the women who were stripping pandanas leaves and laying out the cured strands to be added to the ten-meter-long mat they were weaving for the King's birthday feast. Larry joined several of the fishermen on a five-mile journey across to the volcano to deliver two pigs which had to be shoved

Jan Metherall and I may have been responsible for introducing popcorn to these people. On games day children and adults eagerly devoured five garbage bagsful of fresh popcorn. (The only blond head here belongs to Brendan Metherall.)

off the boat and guided by swimmers onto a wave-washed landing rock. We had both walked to the small plantations owned by individual families on the southern side of the island to help load the only community-owned truck with coconuts and bananas. We learned that this was a cash-poor island, the only income coming from the mats woven of flax and pandanas leaves which the women cut then soaked in the sea to bleach and make them supple and from highly condensed lemon juice. The mats woven here were of particularly fine quality and highly sought after by Tongans on the other islands of this small nation and from those living overseas where they were used for ceremonial purposes.

There was no tourism here. No scheduled air flights as the only plane that flew in to the tiny airstrip brought occasional officials to do a quick inspection or have a short stay in the small cottage kept ready and waiting next to the Capitol building. There was little to buy other than bread baked in a stone ovens in front of the baker's house plus some batteries and simple food stuffs sold from shops that had no signs – the islanders all knew which home they were in. With the only cargo arriving once every six weeks if the weather and also the condition of the Tongan ferry allowed, the islanders depended on fish plus the abundant tropical fruits and root vegetables which thrived on the rich volcanic soil away from the coral sand shores up the sides of the 500-foot-high ridge of hills that crowned Niuatoputapu. Keini described how, when at times the ferry didn't arrive from Neiafu, the local supplies of flour ran out, as did oil and everyone's favorite treat – canned corn beef.

"Boy do we get tired of fish and yams then," she added.

Only for truly special occasions was one of the dozens of pigs that wandered freely along the foreshore slaughtered. And the day before we planned to set sail one very small piglet was sacrificed so a feast could be prepared for us and the Metheralls by the families of Keini and Mele.

The rich aroma of roasting pork greeted us as we approached Mele's family home, Jan bearing a large chocolate cake she'd baked that morning, Larry carrying two jars of honey and some embroidered towels for Mele's mother, plus several lengths of ribbon which we knew the girls would use to decorate their luxurious hair. Fragrant smoke rose from where a half dozen men where retrieving parcels of food that had been wrapped in banana leaves and slowly baked in a stone-lined pit in the ground, just in front of a small cooking shelter set well away from the other buildings. We were quickly escorted into dining area. After the blazing heat of early afternoon, this space offered a welcome cool respite, its walls woven from pandanas leaves and decorated with large sheets of tapa cloth, the floor covered with long lengths of locally woven mats, large doors built to let in the tradewind breezes, fronted by porches shaded with palm fronds. A line of women and children paraded through the doors, bringing parcel after parcel of steaming banana leaves which they placed along the center of the mats. As soon as we were seated cross-legged on the floor with a plate set in front of us, each parcel was ceremoniously opened – taro, yams, whole fish steamed in coconut milk, chicken pieces coated with coconut oil, palm hearts steamed with a variety of shell fish, and a dish I'd never have expected to find delectable: good old-fashioned canned corn beef, mixed with thinly shredded local greens and baked with coconut milk.

The exotic aromas filled the air. A big pitcher of freshly squeezed juice, almost solid with the pulp of the tropical fruits stood surrounded by an assortment of jars and glasses. We seven visitors politely waited for everyone else to sit down. Nothing happened. Instead all the adults continued to stand quietly around the edges of the room, the children and teenagers looking in from the doorways. I heard some giggles and saw Mele come just inside the room to whisper to her mother. Then Keini came over and leaned down to where we sat.

"You must take some food. You must eat first," she explained. "When you are finished everyone else can eat too."

Keini immediately left to join the younger folks outside the house. As soon as we began taking samples of each dish, the serious mood lightened, especially whenever one or the other of us indicated something was particularly tasty. The youngest guest, Bridgette, pushed the first bits of food around on her plate for a few seconds before glancing towards her mother then taking a small bite of whelks roasted with seaweed, breadfruit and coconut milk. She didn't hesitate before reaching for more. Her brothers immediately followed suit. Though several of the dishes must have been unfamiliar looking, and the aromas exotic, all three children tried at least a small spoonful of each dish on offer. I was not surprised at the way the Metherall children handled the awkwardness of being watched by two dozen people while they ate because I have noticed, through our years of voyaging, how youngsters who spent time cruising with their parents learned to be comfortable in unusual situations.

As soon as "the guests" finished the first serving of each dish, the adults joined us. When they had settled back away from the eating mat after finishing their meal, the food that was left was carried out to be shared among the children. The formality and any shyness evaporated with the meal. Our tasty cool drinks were replenished time and again as the afternoon light began to fade. When we finally stood to leave, Mele's mother began rolling up the twelve-foot-long finely woven mat that been the centerpiece of the eating area. She called to Mele and after a hurried conversation presented the mat to me.

"My mother wants you to remember us each time you eat off this mat," Mele translated. "She wants you to know when you come back you are always welcome in our home."

That mat became a cherished memento of our very first Tongan feast. In fact, it is mounted along the length of the wall next to my desk as I write these words.

Before we'd set sail from the US, a friend who had lived in Tonga many years before had suggested we buy guitar strings as possible gifts for people who might befriend us. Since I wanted some spares on board for my guitar, I'd bought an extra half dozen just in case. Now, I'd brought three sets ashore with me and before we headed back to *Taleisin*, I asked Mele and Keini to walk with me to the home of the school teacher. The delight with which the teacher accepted the guitar strings showed how right my friend had been.

As we shook his hand and prepared to leave, he commented, "Holiday time is over tomorrow. Children will all be back in school so I have to finish preparing more lessons."

Later, we reflected on our good fortune – how we happened to arrive in time for the school holidays, how the children were the ones to introduce us to their culture. As we finished stowing two crates containing gifts of fruit and bottles of condensed lemon juice we'd been asked to take to relatives in Vava'u, then lifted *Cheeky* on board in preparation for an early morning departure, Larry said to me, "Can you believe our timing? What luck to sail here just after the pass was blown through the reef, and then to arrive when all the kids were out of school. It was the kids that made it so easy to break the ice with these folks."

I agreed with him, of course. But as our Tongan sojourn continued I realized it was not just good timing or luck that had made our visit special. During his first visit here in 1773, Captain James Cook had found the reception so congenial he marked his chart of these waters with *The Friendly Isles*. Over the next two months, as we came to know the more easily accessible parts of Tonga, we learned the name still is an almost perfect fit.

Some of my best memories from the Friendly Isles are of afternoons spent working together with a group of local women, making mats that are an integral part of life here. Some of these mats are used every day; others are for ceremonial purposes.

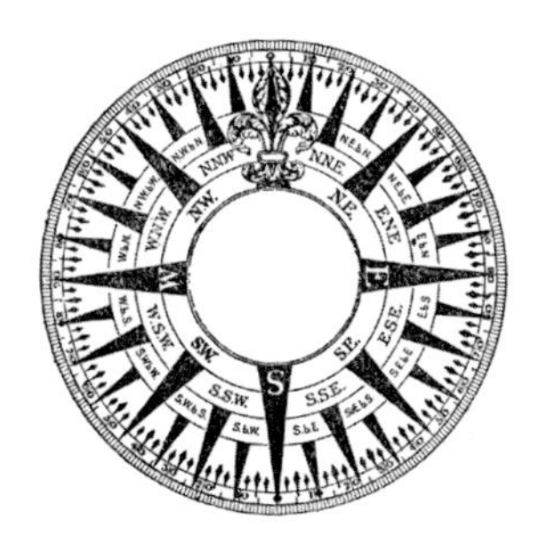

CHAPTER 8

THE FRIENDLY ISLES, PART II

Though we have a relatively long list of favorite voyaging destinations, there are only a few places that offer what I would call perfect cruising. The waters around La Paz in Mexico's Baja California, Brazil's Isla Grande, the Aland Islands in Finland: each has an easily accessible, small but bustling town where we could anchor safely to re-provision, enjoy the delights of ice cream stands, cafés and a bit of night life and savor the taste of being in a foreign country. Each has nearby islands with a variety of anchorages – some we shared with other cruising sailors, some where we met local folks, others where we were completely on our own. And the sailing between the islands and the relatively central town was in sheltered waters. In each place we'd linger for a few months exploring the islands, then return to town to re-provision and spend time amidst the hustle and bustle, then lift our anchor again to sail for a few hours to reach a new anchorage or return to one we'd previously enjoyed. These places were like a refreshing pause to us, a break from the normal voyaging rhythm which forces you to keep moving onward due to schedules imposed by the changing seasons,

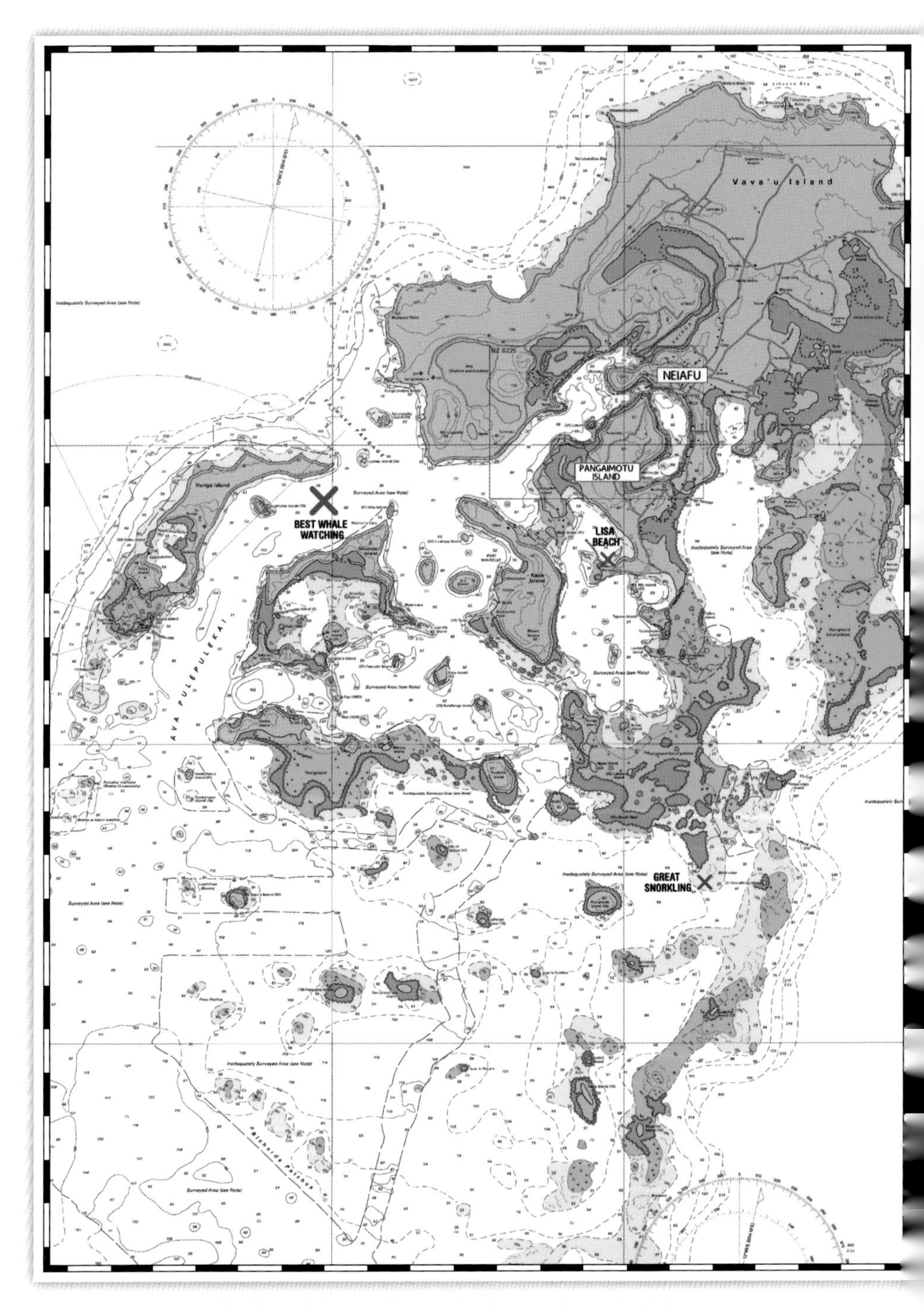

The archipelago of Vava'u. We meandered among these islands for almost two months. Our family's plantation is just to the northeast of Lisa Beach.

the threat of cyclones or icy winter storms. And in each we met people who became life-long friends.

From the moment we sailed out of the open ocean and into the sheltered waterways leading through the Islands of Vava'u towards Neiafu, the clearance port for Northern Tonga, we sensed we would add another perfect cruising destination to the list.

You could say the deck was stacked in our favor long before we reached Vava'u. Meeting some of the local people was going to be easy since we were carrying two crates of gifts to deliver for our friends from Niuatoputapu. One crate was for a cousin named Leonati who dispensed fuel at the tiny boatyard near where we anchored, and who sold his whale bone and wood carvings in the craft shop and sailors' hangout, above the boatyard office. The other crate was for Keini's aunt Sanaae and uncle Tani Hausia on Pangai Motu, an island just three miles south and connected by bridge to Neiafu. By coincidence, Bob Ramirez, the same Californian friend who suggested we bring guitar strings as potential gifts, had also given us money to purchase something to take along to Sanaae and Tani. Bob had been working his way around the world for almost eight years, when he hitchhiked to Tonga on board a sailboat. There he met and fell in love with Catharina, the oldest and, many say, the most beautiful of the Hausia daughters. Bob had stayed with the family, helping on their small plantation for several months and wooing Catharina – only to lose out to a Canadian sailor who actually owned his own boat. In spite of leaving without one of the Hausia daughters as his bride, Bob had fond memories of Sanaae and Tani and hoped his gift would help introduce us to their special warmth.

Many years before, during our first year of cruising on *Seraffyn*, Larry had seen me admiring some handmade Mexican crafts – necklaces, placemats, embroidered shirts, pottery – as we walked through the marketplace in La Paz.

"Why don't you buy something?" he'd suggested. "Wonderful colors. You'd look good in that one."

I'd reminded him that our budget was somewhat limited and the storage space on board *Seraffyn* even more so. Two days later Larry brought me an empty generous-sized cardboard shoe box.

"Can you find space for this in one of your lockers?" he asked.

"Of course. But why should I?"

"Because you love having some of the local crafts, looking at them. And you should make room to carry some along with you. I suggest from now on you buy as many handicraft items as you can fit in this box. Knowing you, you'll give them away as gifts somewhere down the line. Folks will love them because something nice from Mexico will seem exotic to someone in Panama or wherever we might sail."

He had been right. And through all the years of our voyaging, that box (and the sturdier and slightly larger plastic ones that replaced it) never overflowed but always held an interesting selection of items of varying value. I enjoyed searching these handicrafts out and they made interesting gifts for unexpected birthdays among the cruising fleet, or as thank-you gifts for people who befriended us, or for occasions such as this.

Three days after we anchored in Neiafu, I took a hand-painted ironstone Mexican vase from the gift box, then added a few of the silk frangipani flowers I'd bought from a roadside stand in Bora Bora. I wrapped them, along with Bob's letter, in the brightly colored wrapping paper I kept under the gift box. We rowed ashore and walked leisurely towards Pangai Motu. We knew the Hausia family would have heard a bit about us by now as the box of produce we'd brought from Niuatoputapu had already been delivered by Leonati. So we weren't surprised when, directed by various children along our way, we arrived at the Hausia family home – a beautiful plot with a modest, two-roomed concrete walled house and a separate cookhouse, surrounded by picturesque banana trees – to be welcomed with, "Hello Mrs Leen, Mr Larry." What did surprise us was the reaction our gift caused. At first I thought it was the beauty of the vase and flowers which made Sanaae shriek with delight and call out to her three daughters who were waiting politely in the shade near the cookhouse. But then Sanaae carefully set the vase aside and soon I realized it was Bob's letter she found most intriguing.

"He fought very hard for my sister," Suidi, the second oldest of the girls, told us. "My mother says the fight was really dramatic."

She described how Sanaae liked both of the suitors but was prejudiced towards Bob because he had literally lived beneath her roof, on a mat in the boys' room, and become like family, learning to speak Tongan, helping with the harvest. And from this close living she came to understand that Bob owned nothing but what he wore, had no profession other than world wanderer, while Peter, in contrast, owned a nice sailboat which he'd sailed from Canada and was a professional chef with a good career to return to.

"And now," Suidi continued, "though Catarina lives in Canada, far away from us, she is happy and well cared for. But Mom wants to know about Bob. And she wants you to bring your boat closer to here so she can make you a feast; you can come to church with us on Sunday, and you can be here when we pound the tapa cloth and Ponove can take Larry fishing and…"

Only minutes after we rowed home to *Taleisin*, Peter Metherall came over from where *Pegasus* lay anchored, about 200 yards further up the bay. "Made friends with the Kiwi sailors from those two boats," Peter said. "They've heard of a family that puts on a Tongan feast with traditional music and dancing in another bay if at least twelve people join in. My family is up for it; that makes nine of us. What about you two? How about we all race over there on Saturday?"

The anchorage they described, one which cruising sailors called Lisa Beach, was right where we wanted to be, next to the plantation owned by "our family," the Hausias.

"Why don't we try to get a few more cruisers to come along? Make it a staggered start, first boat in is the winner," I suggested. "Charge each entrant two beers. We can use the beer as the prizes for first boats to finish. That might entice more folks to join in."

Peter agreed to row around and invite the crews of all of the boats anchored to port of us; Larry agreed to invite all the crews to starboard.[1]

Racing is not everyone's idea of fun, and several of the female partners on boats Larry visited agreed only when Larry emphasized this was just a casual affair with the racing not to be taken too seriously. So by the time we convened the "committee meeting" the next morning, the majority of the boats around us went on the starting list. Peter and Larry began debating how to rate such disparate boats so all would have a fair chance of winning their share of the beer.

I looked over the list of entrants, then asked, "Don't the folks on that big yacht want to come along?"

"When I rowed past them no one seemed to be on board," Larry said. "Besides, that's probably a charter boat – professional skipper, cook. I'd guess it's being used by some wealthy industrialist who wants peace and quiet and wouldn't be interested."

I climbed into *Cheeky* and rowed over to the elegant 85-footer. The carefully groomed skipper came out on deck when I came alongside and listened politely to my invitation.

"If it was my boat, we'd be up for it, but not sure my owner would be interested. If you can wait a few minutes, I'll ask him."

---

1 In 1985 when we first visited Neiafu, the two or three dozen visiting yachts all lay to their own anchors in 80 to 90 feet of water. There were only a few moorings in front of the town for the charter fleet of about a dozen boats. During our later visits many moorings had been laid and were available for a reasonable fee, but there still was plenty of room to anchor.

Tim, Brendan and Bridgette Metherall were enthusiastic and skilled crew as we raced against a fleet of fourteen other cruising boats from Neiafu to Lisa Beach.

Henry Heinz, the retired chairman of Heinz 57 Corporation, came on deck moments later. "What a grand idea. I have a complete office on board. You'll need to hand out race instructions; you can use my Xerox machine to make copies. And since we will obviously be the last boat to set off, my crew can be the starting committee."

The three Metherall youngsters joined us the next morning to act as crew, first rowing around the anchorage and handing out the xeroxed race instructions, then returning to help winch up 300 feet of anchor chain as Larry and I hoisted the sails. Though all of the fifteen entrants had agreed this was supposed to be a casual race, the casualness seemed to disappear as soon as first one boat then another sailed past the start flags. The sailing weather was perfect: fifteen-knot tradewinds, no sea at all as our course led us running or reaching through the maze of islands. Good-natured joking could be heard between competitors as they looked for opportunities to overtake each other. Larry was relaxed as he guided the boat towards where he spotted patches of slightly fresher winds, quietly suggesting sail adjustments, eagerly pointing out potential anchorages and diving spots he wanted to come back to. He didn't object when I suggested stringing up the cockpit awning we used for cruising, something I'd never have suggested when we were competing in more formally organized races. Our crew became ever more comfortable with their roles on board. But it was when we had to tighten up our sheets as we passed Kapa Island then beat towards Lisa Beach on Pangai Motu that, for our crew, the real fun began – and I was reminded of Larry's sometimes overly competitive nature.

We'd caught up with a few of the boats that had started before us. Now only two yachts were ahead of us. Michelle and Russell Minto, two Australians sailing their Adams designed 40-footer, *Last Wave,* were very slowly overtaking us. A mine field of coral heads lay just ahead. Russell drove *Last Wave* within a half dozen boat lengths of the coral heads.

"Get ready to tack," I heard him call to Michelle.

Michelle had previously mentioned she didn't particularly want to race, just to come along for the feast. So I was surprised to hear her loudly urging Russell, "Don't tack. They'll get away from us."

I laughed and called to her, "Don't worry, we have to tack too," then began organizing our young crew. "Brendan, can you go up on the foredeck and make sure the jib clears the staysail stay when we come about? Bridget, you handle the jib sheet."

But Larry, who had assured everyone this was just a casual race, firmly stated, "Don't say a word and don't do anything. We aren't going to tack. I can see clear water between those coral heads."

"We can't sail through there," I said, alarm obvious in my voice.

"Lin, go up on the foredeck yourself and keep a close watch. I'm not tacking unless we are actually going to hit something."

Already there was a coral head between *Last Wave* and us. I rushed forward and looked around.

"Larry, we've got to tack," I said as we skimmed by, our keel in deep water, the ragged arms of coral reaching right to the surface just a few feet from our starboard side.

"Don't look to port or starboard, just look straight ahead," Larry stated firmly as *Taleisin* plowed onward. "Stop worrying, Lin. No swell; I can see clear water in another 100 yards. Just find me a path between the next coral heads."

A few dozen yards to starboard, Russell was waving his fist at us. "You crazy fools," he yelled as *Last Wave* bore away on an offshore tack and we sailed clear of the coral and into the lead. Our excited young crew whooped with delight as we eased *Taleisin*'s sheets to reach across the last few miles of water towards our destination. My heart was pounding madly as I looked behind us to see the bomb field of coral heads.[2] Then I began to laugh at the craziness racing brought out in Larry but also at the fact that in my heart of hearts I'd really loved those moments of madness. I came back to the cockpit chuckling as I pointed to windward. There, looking stately and handsome, moving swiftly past *Last Wave* and then past us with thousands of square feet of sail set, was Mr Heinz and his elegant craft which had started the race almost a half hour after the last boat had left, and was now clearly taking the lead and the honors.

Just as I have seen at least a hundred times before, the crowd of relative strangers that landed on the beach had gained a mutuality, a sense of camaraderie that grew as each of the day's racing details were dissected, rehashed and replayed.

"Best day I've had in years," Henry Heinz enthused as he was presented with half of the beers as first boat to finish, beers he accepted almost as formally and proudly as if this had been an international event (which in a way it was!). "I told Brian I had important business to take care of. But I also told him to call me each time we caught up with another boat. After we passed the first few boats, I forgot about work and took over the helm myself."

Along with the rest of us, Henry Heinz settled down on the mats our feast hosts had laid along the sandy shore, as we all were urged to open

2 Also known as "bommies," a term coined by Australian surfers for sea waves over shallows, the nickname originating from the indigenous Australian word "bombora."

the steaming parcels that began emerging from the rock lined roasting pit. Three Tongan men strummed on battered guitars as we ate, the unfamiliar tunes and foreign words sweet with harmony as one voice rang in a high falsetto, another boomed an underlying base. Then four young women, their golden-hued skin gleaming through a coating of coconut oil, walked gracefully from where they had been waiting under the coconut palms behind us. Each was barefoot, their waists wrapped in woven matting, their hair decorated with flowers. The women knelt on a mat set between us and the gently lapping wavelets of the bay and began dancing with only their upper bodies and arms as they used their hands to illustrate the story being sung by the guitarists.

The sailors who'd shared the day with us slowly grew silent, mesmerized as I was by the music, the glowing colors of sunset reflecting off the still water of the bay. I looked around at this assortment of sailors from seven different countries, each voyaging on vastly different boats, ranging from 25 feet to 85 feet in length, each with different financial circumstances and different goals, yet united for these few hours by the feeling that we were all exactly where we were supposed to be.

I didn't get to lie in the next morning.

Ponove, the second oldest Hausia son, was calling from the shore. "We must go diving now and bring Mrs Leen ashore because my mother is waiting to make her a shirt."

His planning suited me perfectly. It meant Larry could spend a whole day doing what he loved almost as much as sailing, while I would be able to stay out of the sun and wind and water while I did what I truly enjoy: getting to know how other people live.

Larry often expressed his annoyance when he heard me say to a new acquaintance, "I don't really like the water, nor the sun, nor the wind."

"That sounds kind of dumb, Lin, because here you are out wandering around on a sailboat," he would say, shaking his head.

"But I love sailing," I would answer. "Using the wind to move my home across an ocean, going new places, meeting all sorts of new people, having adventures."

As a young person all my favorite pursuits had been indoor ones; music, debate squad, reading everything and anything, card competitions like bridge (though not writing – something that as a youth I did only under duress). It was when I met Larry that that I was introduced to sailing. And with my fair skin and light eye coloring I burned easily, no matter how much sunblock I slathered on myself. With my long hair and the broad-brimmed hats I prefer wearing, I didn't particularly enjoy being out in the wind. That is why I became the chief navigator, bosun and cook and, except on watch, tended to find reasons to stay below decks. And, in spite of being a relatively good swimmer, I have always been uncomfortable swimming in the ocean, probably because my early swimming days had been in crystal clear California swimming pools where I knew exactly what was in the water with me. Though I was willing to climb overboard and swim close to the boat to cool off, or to spend fifteen or twenty minutes snorkeling along the edges of tropical reefs, I only went along while Larry was skin-diving to keep him company. And when I did, I ended up spending a lot of my time feeling windblown and roasted in the dinghy as I waited for him to tire of meandering around under water and spear a fish for our dinner.

And so, I was perfectly happy that Suidi was waiting for me when we rowed ashore. As the two men rowed back towards *Taleisin,* I heard Ponove suggest Larry put the outboard motor on *Cheeky* so they could get to the outer reefs. Then he said the words I knew would hook Larry: "We can get some lobster out there."

Suidi took my hand to lead me away from the beach and through the ranks of coconut palms that lined the foreshore, up a gentle slope past carefully tended vanilla bean and pineapple plants and onto a clear grassy plateau where two woven huts were set well clear of all the trees.

"Don't expect them to come home until it is almost dark," Suidi said just before she led me into the larger of the two huts. "Ponove will take Larry to drink some kava with his friend on the island near the outer reef, then they'll go search for lobster all day out there. Probably just come home with some fish. But that means you can stay with me."

She led me into the larger hut where a dozen girls and women sat cross-legged on the mat-covered floor, some mending clothes or sewing shirts or taking turns at an antique-looking pedal sewing machine, others weaving baskets or mats, still others slicing lengths of pandanas or flax leaves. I settled in to a spot the women cleared for me. Then Sanaae came over and, without the least bit of awkwardness, handed me a bundle of pandanas leaves along with the lid off a tin can and demonstrated how I should use the edge of the lid to slice pandanas. As I tried slicing off some preliminary strips, she deftly took a few measurements and set to work cutting shirt parts from a length of brightly colored cloth. Sixteen-year-old Suidi and her older sister Mary were in a constant state of giggles as they helped me learn the names (and correct pronunciations) of the

Tani Hausia squeezes the milk from grated coconuts in preparation for dinner.

women around me, their relationship to each other, their role within the community. The girls acted as translators as I answered a deluge of questions about where I came from, where I was going, why I didn't have children. The last question caused a burst of laughter and chatter. Suidi was a bit hesitant to translate but then she pointed at one of the women who had danced so gracefully the day before.

"Lisa says there definitely doesn't look like there is anything wrong with your husband. She thinks he's really sexy."

I couldn't contain my laughter, which seemed to break any last barriers. "Absolutely nothing wrong with him," I answered when I stopped laughing. "We just haven't been blessed with kids."

And with that the door was open for my own set of inquiries – questions

The marketplace at Neiafu was small. To get the best choice I tried to be ashore by 0900. We'd sail to town once every week or ten days to buy fresh provisions, enjoy the local cafés then head out to explore yet another island or rejoin our Tongan family.

that had been bubbling up in me.

It was late afternoon when Larry and Ponove returned with just one lobster but enough fresh fish to share with the whole family. By then my head was spinning from all the stories I'd been told, the homes I'd been taken to visit. As Larry and I rowed back to *Taliesin* with the lobster – which everyone insisted should be our dinner – I tried to share what I'd learned that day, telling him how each Tongan family was given ownership of a small plot of land to build a house in the village where they were born, plus a generous piece of land outside the village to cultivate food and cash crops like vanilla, pineapple and copra, but how few actually lived on what was locally termed the plantation.

"Too lonely," Sanaae had explained. "Newlyweds like Ponove and Lisa sometimes live out here until they have two or three children. But then the wife gets lonely and wants to be with all of us."

Earlier that day, when Sanaae had finished the handsome shirt which she insisted I wear, we'd walked the half mile from the plantation to Sanaae's village home with its new-looking block walls and small windows. Tani insisted Suidi translate carefully as he showed me the most important feature of what to me appeared to be a far less inviting house than the sweet-smelling woven hut on the plantation. He led me through the two main rooms and into what looked like a pantry. Then he pulled open a large trap door. There, down a short flight of stairs, was a cyclone shelter big enough for the whole extended Hausia family plus a few barrels of water and food.

"I have seen many cyclones in my life," Tani had explained as Suidi translated. "But last year, only three days after my first grandchild was born, the worst cyclone ever crossed right over my home. We did everything we could to be prepared, tied rocks to the roof, put extra bindings on the woven walls, made sure everything in the yard was tied down. But when the heaviest winds and rain hit, I felt the walls of my house being ripped away, the rain and wind destroying everything inside. I had to run through the storm with my grandson in my arms while sheets of roofing metal came flying past me. I made it safely to the school house – it has solid block walls and was already overflowing with people. I had to take care of the baby and I didn't know where the rest of my family was until the next day. When we went back to our house there was almost nothing left. Then the church and Red Cross came and offered to help us build solid houses. I took out a loan, pledging all that we had. I wrote to my brother who works in the United States. He sent some money. It will take us all years to finish paying for all the bricks and cement. It won't matter if the houses on the plantation blow away. We can always build some more. What matters is now I can gather every one of my family right here where I can take care of them."

"Sounds like you had an interesting day," Larry said as I began heating water to steam the two-pound lobster. "Ponove was a hoot, can swim like a fish. I lent him your diving fins. Hope you don't mind. He thinks you would enjoy going across to meet his cousin who lives on Kapa Island tomorrow."

Then he looked at me intently. It was a look I was familiar with; Larry had a plan.

"Lin, there seems to be so much to do around here. I don't feel like moving on just so we can see Fiji. And now this – Tani's story. That really has me convinced. We have to get south before cyclone season. That

I always felt a little sad seeing the tiny piglets slaughtered and roasted to provide special meals for us. But our Tongan family really enjoyed the rare chance to share what to them is a holiday treat.

means we've only got five or six weeks to spend. How about spending it around here? We can sail to Fiji next season if we want."

I was in full accord. Though it is tempting to try to visit as many places as possible during the weather-stipulated cruising season, our best memories were built when we forgot schedules and took time to get to know one place well.

The next day when I mentioned we were planning to stay in Vava'u, Sanaae clapped her hands and said, "Good, now you can become part of the Hausia family."

Our lives fell into a comfortable rhythm. We spent several days each week at anchor near the family plantation where *Taleisin* seemed to become just one more part of the Hausia family home, her foredeck a perfect diving platform for youngsters, her shaded cockpit an evening refuge for a half dozen adults. Most mornings Larry and I spent together doing small boat maintenance jobs, adding a fresh coat of varnish to *Taleisin*'s spars, painting her bulwarks so she would look fresh and smart when we headed to New Zealand. Afternoons we were enfolded into the daily lives of our "Tongan family," joining them as they worked the plantation or socialized with their friends.

Sometimes cruisers we'd met in other countries sailed in to anchor nearby. Ponove insisted we bring them along to family gatherings. "Your friends are our friends too," he'd say.

Every six or seven days we'd sail back to Neiafu where we spent our mornings slowly gathering provisions for our voyage south and afternoons socializing with other sailors and the ex-pat yachtsmen who had opened small businesses in the main port town. Sometimes one or another of the Hausia family came to town to seek us out, and every Sunday Suidi was waiting on shore, be it at Pangai Mōtu or in Neiafu, with Ponove and the family taxi he drove, to take us to church, followed by a leisurely family dinner. Sundays were part of our ritual; even if the religious aspects of the ceremony did not move us personally, we enjoyed attending the social gathering, for the wonderful harmonic singing, and for the view it gave us of local life – and, mostly, because it seemed to please Sanaae and Tani so much.

We learned about local traditions and the importance Tongans place on family in other ways, too – sometimes indirectly. One such enlightening experience came through our acquaintanceship with Robyn Coleman,

A reminder of the reason prudent cruisers head to higher latitudes for the cyclone season, this boat was built by a Tongan family completely of salvaged parts from cyclone-wrecked yachts. They use it to commute between Kapa Island and Neiafu.

who had sailed to Tonga with her husband Dave and two children almost seven years before. Dave, an experienced deep sea diver, began a tourist diving company and took over the small run-down boatyard carved into the cliff just below the main street of Neiafu. Robyn, a highly gregarious woman, began a co-op to help the local women sell their crafts to visiting sailors. She was a fountain of knowledge about Tongan life. On our way to lunch with her during one of our days in town, Larry noticed a diving knife he'd given Ponove the previous week – only it was sported not by Ponove but by one of his friends, who was walking along the dusty main street of town with the knife strapped to his ankle. Larry looked perplexed.

"Ponove had been admiring my knife, kept borrowing it while we were diving together," Larry told me. "I gave it to him because I can easily replace it when we get to New Zealand."

At lunch, Larry happened to mention this to Robyn, adding, "I am a bit disappointed. Thought Ponove really wanted it."

Robyn was quick to reassure Larry. "He probably treasured it, showed it to all his friends. Even told me about it. But if you are Tongan and a friend or family member admires something, you get kudos by giving it to them gracefully. Possessions aren't regarded in the same way among most of the Polynesian people I've met as they are among us Palangis. What matters to these people are their family and their place within their community."

Five weeks after we'd arrived in Vava'u, a low pressure system developed into a tropical storm just 200 miles to the east of Neiafu. Though it dissipated before it reached Tonga, Tani's tale of the devastating power of cyclones was in the back of our minds as we made one last foray into town to buy a supply of fresh food, get our clearance papers and pay the very small departure tax. Ponove and his wife Lisa came on board for dinner while we were in Neiafu.

"We are going to set sail Saturday morning," Larry told them. "Planning to walk out to Pangai Motu and say good-bye to your parents tomorrow, then pick up our papers and leave the next day."

"You must sail to Pangai Motu so my family can make you a farewell feast," Ponove insisted.

We explained we could only get our papers on a weekday and had to leave immediately afterwards. We were sorry, but we would have to forego the feast.

Ponove's eyes twinkled. "Don't worry," he said. "I will fix that."

Sure enough, the official, who turned out to be another cousin of the Hausia family, told us we could leave any time on Saturday and must sail to Pangai Motu, emphasizing we could only anchor there and nowhere else before departing southward but placing no time limit on our stop-over near the family plantation.

It was late Saturday when we sailed in to anchor near the plantation. When we walked up to Sanaae's house she was clearly unhappy. Suidi explained that their church had rules against working on a Sunday – and that preparing a feast, making music and dancing constituted work.

"So we'll make the feast," Larry said.

I thought of the dozen packages of spaghetti we had on board, the packages of frozen ground beef I'd bought for our voyage south, the tins of canned tomatoes we'd carried right across the Pacific. They could be made into spaghetti Bolognese to feed the whole family. As we rowed back out to *Taleisin*, I noticed Mike Green, a sailor we'd become friends with in Neiafu, anchored about a quarter mile to the south. Mike was a professional baker. When we rowed over and suggested he join us and help create a feast for the family, his reaction was exactly as I'd hoped.

"I'll bake some bread and a cake," Mike said without a moment's hesitation.

And so we set to work: Larry and me on *Taleisin*, Mike on *Southwind*.

Tani and Mele Hausia are preparing the pit where they bake feasts for guests.

When we rowed ashore the next day with the prepared food, I learned that, just as the officials had bent the rules to let the Hausia family give us a proper send-off, so had the Catholic priest. When all fifteen of our "family" sat down around the dining mats which were spread across the thick grass in front of the plantation cooking hut, Sanaae directed her daughters to set out the large pot of spaghetti Bolognese and two big bowls of green salad we'd prepared and the long loafs of fresh bread Mike had baked, then she had them open the cooking pit and bring out the food she'd been given special dispensation to cook. Everyone, from the youngest to the oldest, guests and hosts ate together this one time. And when the food bowls were empty and dark had descended, I noticed Lisa whispering first with her mother-in-law, and then with Ponove. She stood up and went into her grass-sided home then came out wearing her dancing costume, carrying Ponove's guitar.

"I am told it is okay to dance on Sunday, only because you will be leaving us tomorrow."

We didn't leave the next day. As we were lifting *Cheeky* on board in preparation for departing, Ponove borrowed a local fisherman's dinghy to row up and tell us we should not believe the weather report; a storm might be coming. Though our barometer was steady and the morning report we'd received over our shortwave radio did not indicate any approaching storm, neither of us could resist the excuse to actually lie in bed and read all day.

The next morning it happened again. Ponove rowed out to state, "You can't leave."

"We are all prepared, the weather looks good. It's time to go," Larry said.

"But you will have bad luck if you leave before noon," Ponove insisted.

He seemed so concerned about our departure that even Larry put aside his impatience. "Okay, we'll wait until noon," he said. "Give me a chance to finish the book I'm reading."

At exactly noon Larry began winching in our anchor chain. Just as I was about to haul up the mainsail, we heard Ponove shouting as he climbed into his borrowed boat. He and Suidi were soon alongside. He opened up a large gunny sack and began pulling out a half dozen beautiful freshly made baskets plus place mats and eating mats.

"My mother and Lisa and Mary and Betty just now finished these. They have been working on them for two weeks. Now you will always have our hearts with you because there is everything you need for your new home."

"This is my home," I said, indicating the boat I stood on.

"But someday you will have a real home," Ponove said. "And your Tongan family will come and visit you."

As our sails filled and *Taleisin* bore away, farewells rang out from our family who stood along the sandy shore. I noticed Larry had tears in his eyes, just as I did.

"This has been the highlight of my year," he said. "I really did feel like part of the family. I can see why it is hard for them to understand that our boat is our home."

"What they can't fathom is the idea of anyone being without a close-knit family near at hand to care for them, to share in the work of everyday life," I answered as I thought of how, in spite of having little materially, the people of this tiny kingdom, the members of my special family, were amazingly wealthy.

And it wasn't until we'd sailed from this perfect cruising destination only to find another that I learned just how perceptive they had been.

The family cooking house where Sanaae and Mele are preparing dinner on the plantation is open-sided and far cooler than the more western-style house which is their full-time home in the village.

I was slightly spooked by this white-tipped shark, which followed us for several hours. It kept banging its nose against the rudder, almost as if it was trying to get to us. But then Larry pointed out that there were several small pilot fish swimming just under the counter of the boat: its true prey.

CHAPTER 9

TOWARDS THE SOUTHERN CROSS

Memories lie. Or should I say, memories can be highly selective. Case in point: our voyage south from Vava'u towards Nuku'alofa then onwards to New Zealand.

I recall the meander through the Ha'apai group as non-eventful, the ocean passage from Nuku'alofa as ranking among the more pleasant of many ocean passages we made, including days of sailing over an almost flat sea, spinnaker set day and night, dinners in the cockpit with long-stemmed wine glasses standing steady. But recently, in preparation for this chapter, I began reading our old log book and was faced with the day-to-day reality of that voyage along the South Pacific convergence zone,[1] out of the tropics,

1 The South Pacific Convergence Zone denotes the area where the southeast trades from easterly moving anticyclones to the south meet with the semi-permanent easterly flow from the eastern South Pacific anticyclone. It generally stretches from the Solomon Islands through Fiji, Samoa and Tonga. Low-level convergence along this band forms

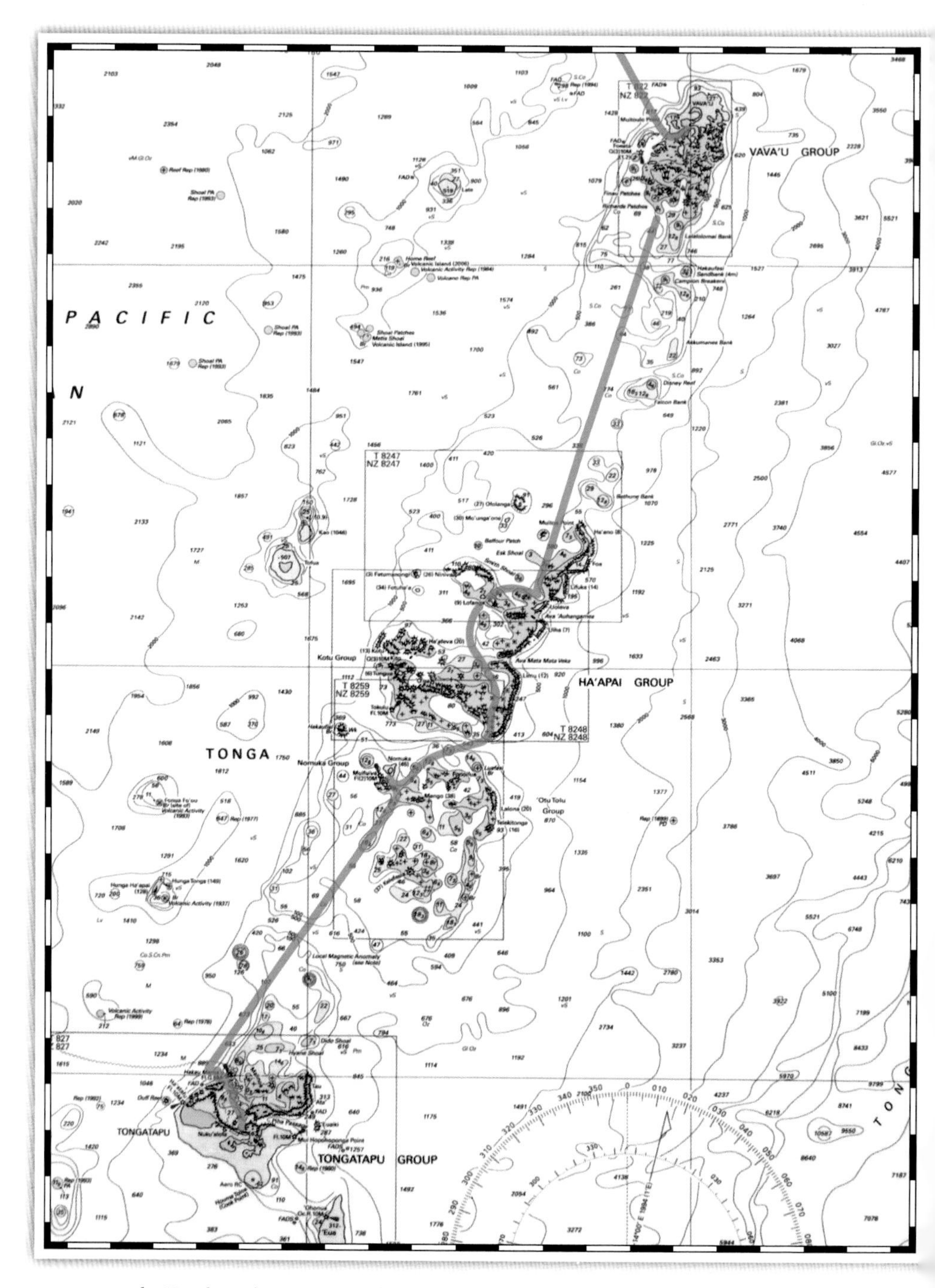

the Kingdom of Tonga is spread over many hundreds of miles of ocean. It is split into three main groups, with outlying islands like Niuatoputapu being as far as 200 miles from their nearest Tongan neighbor.

across the variables of the middle latitudes and into the less predictable weather patterns of the higher latitudes.

From the day Larry and I first launched *Seraffyn*, I began keeping a handwritten logbook. In the beginning the entries were simple notes recording maintenance work we did on the boat, times of departure and arrival, course, speed, sail configurations, anchor depths. But soon I began adding comments about daily happenings so I could share them with my friends and family in the letters I wrote. Later, after Larry and I began writing articles for magazines, my log entries expanded to include impressions, sometimes whole conversations I didn't want to forget. I never begrudged the storage space taken up by our growing collection of logbooks. The information we gleaned from them was so useful we created a special locker when we built *Taleisin*'s interior where we could store previous log books in a waterproof container.

And now, as I re-read each day's entry, I realized how much I had forgotten, for in reality it was only the last four days of our voyage to New Zealand that had, up until now, been lodged so firmly – and pleasantly – in my memory.

By coincidence, we said our final farewells and sailed clear of Pangai Motu on October 31st, Larry's birthday, our wedding anniversary, and exactly two years since the day we launched *Taleisin*. This is also two weeks before the official start of the tropical cyclone season when the South Pacific Convergence Zone tends to be more active over the islands of Tonga. After weeks of mostly sunny skies and tropical warmth, we'd woken to a surprisingly cold drizzle and winds that gusted to 30 knots. For the first time in months, I pulled warm sweaters and long pants from the back of the clothes locker. Though we were eager to get south rather than risk being in the path of any cyclones, I agreed with Larry when, after we'd sailed only ten miles, he suggested anchoring for the night in the shelter of a small unpopulated island to celebrate our anniversary with a quiet dinner and a bottle of sparkling wine from our bilge collection.

We didn't sail onward for several days. It wasn't just the cold blustery weather that kept us at anchor; it was the chance to have the un-interrupted

cloudiness as well as showers and thunderstorms and tends to increase the strength of the tradewinds. The more equatorward portion of the SPCZ is most active in the southern hemisphere summer, and the more poleward portion is most active during transition seasons of fall and spring.

aloneness we both occasionally seem to need. For the first time in several months there were no other cruising friends or adopted family members nearby, no onshore attractions, none of the watch-keeping, navigation or boat-handling duties that are necessary during passages or overnight hops between different islands. We could forget completely about the boat for a while and take our time to relish recapping the experiences we'd just had, talk about what lay ahead, read a book without any distraction or do nothing at all.

When the winds eased back to a more sedate 20 knots, we reached south through the maze of reefs and islands that form the Ha'apai Group of Tonga. Saane had packaged up gifts of fruit and baskets from the plantation for us to deliver to relatives on three different islands in Ha'apai. Normally such a place would tempt us to linger here: the warmth with which our newly acquired relatives greeted us when we arrived with these packages, the interesting diving Larry found along the edges of the reefs, the variety of potential anchorages. But at the back of our minds was the approaching cyclone season. So, after delivering each package, we stayed at anchor through the night then forged onward. It was almost with a sense of relief that we handed the last of Sanaae's packages to its recipient on Nomuka Island and prepared to sail south 60 miles to Tongatapu Island and Nuku'alofa, the capital of Tonga, where we could get our final clearance papers and wait for a relatively clear patch of weather to head towards New Zealand.

Larry was in a rare bad mood. Our anchor windlass had stopped working that morning. I'd been below flaking the chain into its locker and recognized the sound of one of the internal springs breaking because it had happened twice before – and twice Larry had made modifications he was sure would solve the problem. By the time I was on deck, Larry was pulling the last of the chain up hand over hand, cursing silently under his breath.

"One more thing to fix," he grumbled. "Add that to the stitching that is chafing on the lapper, the hose you want replaced on the water tank outlet, the varnish work that's crazing on the cabin sides."

We'd set our lapper and full mainsail to run clear of the anchorage near Nomuka (this is the island where Captain Bligh took on fresh water the day before his crew mutinied and set him adrift in the *Bounty*'s lifeboat.) A few miles later, when I charted our course and told Larry we'd have to head up onto a tight reach, Larry's mood got even darker.

"Give me my foul weather gear," he snapped back at me. "Add 'check windvane bearings' to the work list, and stitching on mainsail's reefing tack ring seems to have some chafe on it, so add that too."

I stayed below, out his way other than when I popped out to take

Larry called this the "Wet Bum Express". It is an old whaling boat that was, during our visit, used to transport children from various islands of Ha'apai to the school at Lifuka.

another bearing and update our position, as Larry seemed to do nothing but glumly look for more items that should be checked over before we were to leave Nuku'alofa. Then, about three hours after we set sail the wind began to increase until it was blowing at close to 35 knots. I helped take the jib off the headstay and stuff it into its bag which we kept secured on the foredeck, then tuck a reef into the mainsail and set the staysail. Shortly afterwards, Larry took a noon sight, saying he wanted to brush up since we hadn't needed to use the sextant for almost four months. I added his sight to my computations.

"Larry, will you take another bearing for me," I called from the chart table. "Unless we're off course, seems like we are getting set to the east… Don't want to end up among the reefs north of Nuku'alofa."

"I've been out here in the cockpit all day, making sure we hold a steady course."

I could tell from the exasperated tone in his voice that Larry was ready to explode, so I didn't answer. I just waited and, a minute later, heard him add, "If you are sure we're being set to the east, I'll just ease off ten degrees to make up for it."

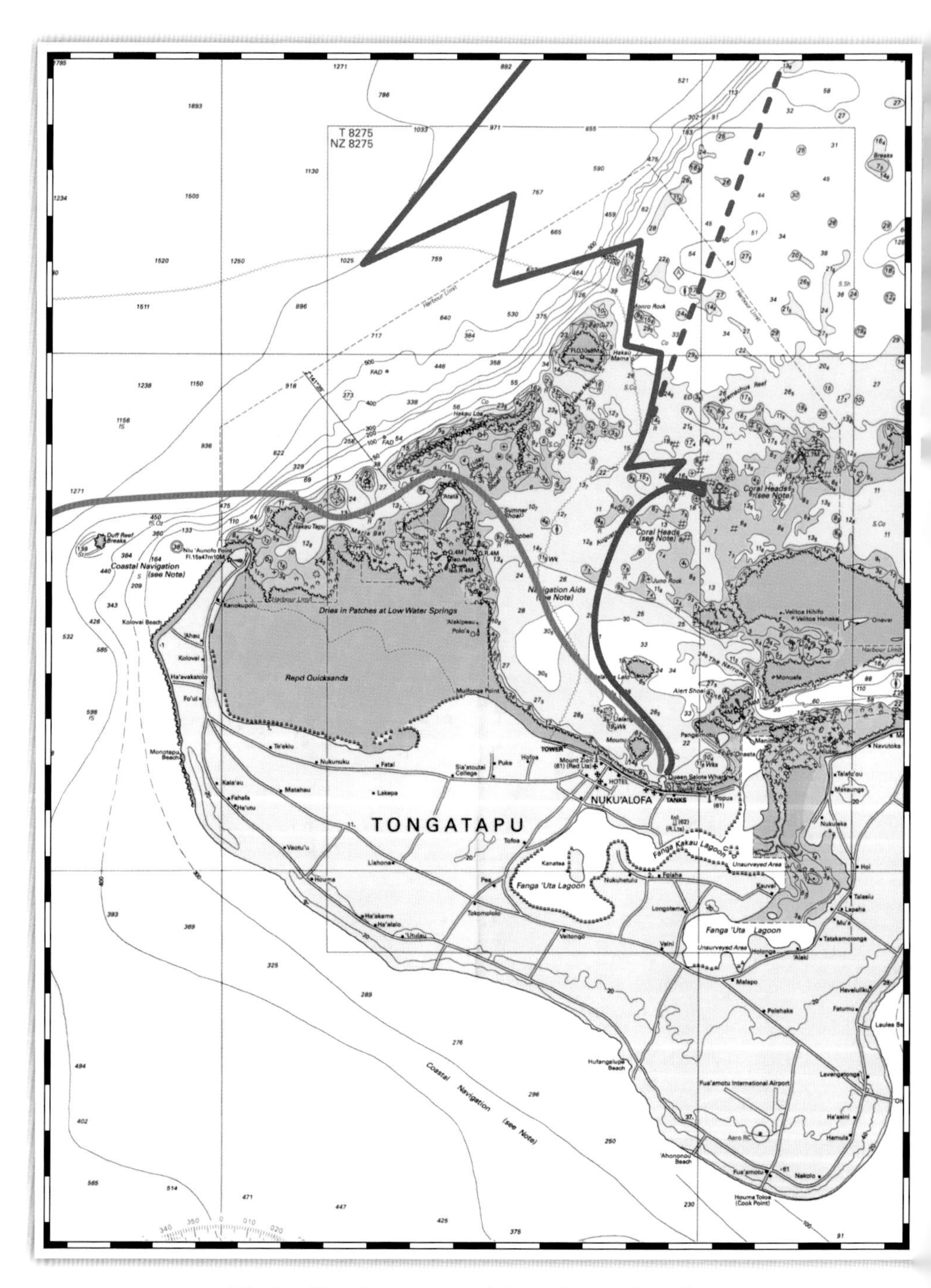

The dotted line shows our intended route between Nomuka and the anchorage of Nuku'alofa. The solid line shows the one we were forced to take due to our technical breakdown. The brown line shows our departure route.

I left him to stew in the cockpit and enjoyed the slightly smoother ride with the sheets eased just a bit. But for some reason I felt uneasy. So an hour later I again went on deck and took a round of bearings off the crest of the volcano that lay northwest of Nomuka, and another off the western end of Tongatapu.

"Larry, my bearings don't make sense," I said. "Can we heave to for a few minutes so I can have a steadier platform? Boat's leaping around a lot. Hard to take bearings, hard to plot them with all this motion."

My suggestion caught Larry's attention. I don't often ask him to stop the boat, but it was a tactic we used whenever one or the other of us wanted to slow things down, think things through. And each time we did Larry jokingly said, "I'd rather be a little late then a lot wrong."

A shower of spray swept across the cockpit as Larry pulled the helm and headed *Taleisin* through the eye of the wind to backwind the staysail and slow the boat down.

"Lin, don't bother to get your foulies on," he said from the cockpit. "You stay down below and I'll use the main compass to take a few bearings. You are probably wasting our time but..."

He left the sails sheeted in tightly and turned the boat to line up with the end of Tongatapu.

When I plotted his bearing on the chart, I felt my stomach drop.

"Larry, if this bearing is right, I was completely wrong about that east-going current. We're way to leeward of where we should be. Can you take another bearing?"

His second bearing confirmed my fears. We'd missed the Tongatapu approaches light by over five miles. We were well to leeward of the reefs we needed to clear, and now we'd have to beat into eight-foot seas on a wind that had us reefed to storm canvas. The roaring, breaking reefs to the south of us caused the marching seas to deflect so that on one tack we were hard on the wind with the seas almost on our beam, but on the other, the seas were almost on our bow. So *Taleisin* plunged and struggled, waves crashing across her foredeck, as we drove her hard in an attempt to get to entrance of the big ships channel before dark. We just made it to the first entrance beacon as dark fell, but still had nine miles to sail through reefs and isolated dangers to reach the relative calm of Nuku'alofa's anchorage.

Then, as we eased sheets to reach past the beacon, Larry noticed the foredeck appeared too clean. It took us both a few minutes to accept that, sometime during that crashing beat, our working jib had been torn loose from its lashings and washed overboard. It was no use going back to look for that jib in the dark. It probably would have sunk like a stone.

Losing that expensive 420-square-foot, two-year-old sail really battered both of our egos, even more than being down to leeward on the 60-mile reach to Nuku'alofa had.

"Bad luck usually runs in threes," I said, trying to lighten the gloom that now enveloped both of us. "The windlass breaking, the navigation problems, the missing jib. Luck should be with us now."

But I was wrong.

Soon after we began tacking up the channel towards the anchorage near the Nuku'alofa, we became lost. I could still see the last lighted buoy of the main ships' channel astern of us, but I couldn't find anything reliable to use as a cross on that bearing.

After a half dozen long tacks I put the chart into a plastic chart case, brought it out into the cockpit and said, "Larry, I want to anchor. I don't feel comfortable about my compass bearings. I feel like we're close to the big coral patches shown right here."

We again hove to while I tried to take bearings to help me distinguish the leading lights and the green light marking the edge of a coral patch that should have been four miles ahead of us. Even with powerful binoculars I couldn't separate the navigation beacons from the confusion of shore lights behind them. Nothing seemed to make sense. By now both of us were feeling not only frustrated but tired. Rain squalls, racing across us and driven by winds that occasionally gusted above gale force, added to our discomfort.

"Okay, I quit," Larry said in a discouraged voice. "Just drop the god-damned sails, drop the damned anchor."

I got out our battery-powered spotlight and shown it right around us. Even with the driving rain I could see there were no dangers within 100 yards of us. Reefs four miles to windward of us were breaking down the ocean swell but still there was about three feet of wind chop. Yet it was with a huge sense of relief that I felt the anchor grab hold soon after Larry let out all 300 feet of chain in 120 feet of water. Dinner was a cup of hot soup and silence as the boat bucked and rolled. Even as we climbed into the two pilot berths and secured the lee-cloths, neither of us said much. We spent an uncomfortable night rolling and lunging, but at least we and the boat were safe.

Sometime during that long night I got up and wrote in the logbook that I was ticked off at Larry because he instantly fell asleep behind his lee cloth in the starboard pilot berth while I lay awake behind my lee cloth almost half the night trying to figure out what we were doing wrong.

By morning the wind had lightened to a more comfortable 20 knots, and the rain had cleared. The mood on board, if not happy, was at least more comfortable as first Larry then I tried to rationalize all the mishaps of the previous day.

"My fault that jib got lost," I said when I tugged on what was left of the lashings on the foredeck. "These lines are really rotten. Been out in the sun too long. I should have checked them."

"Not your fault," Larry countered. "I should have put the jib in the lazarette. Crazy to leave it on deck in that kind of weather. Been thinking about the windlass, and I have an idea of how to fix it."

"With this horrid weather, David and Doreen might still be here. They said they were headed here directly from Neiafu. He was complaining of having too many headsails on board. Maybe we can borrow one and return it when we all get to New Zealand," I added as we took turns leading a nipping line from the anchor chain to a cockpit winch, cranking in the 25 feet of line, feeding 25 feet of chain into the locker then re-leading the nipping line again.

With daylight, it was easy to spot the coral patches and negotiate our way safely into the anchorage. We stayed anchored near the Tongan capital for seven days while we waited for a better patch of weather to head southward. During that time we checked off most of the items on the worklist. We spent a lot of this time licking our wounded egos, looking for errors in in my plotting and the bearings I'd taken with the handbearing compass. After a few days Larry reminded me of the agreement we'd made years before, almost like a wedding vow: share the credit, share the blame.

"I should have checked over your piloting the first time you voiced any doubts. If I hadn't been in such a bad mood, I probably would have. So put the charts away; no answers there. We just have got to be more careful, got to stay to windward."

But I still felt puzzled by what I jokingly called our Tongan jinx, and plagued by the feeling that somehow our sailing lives were slightly out of control.

When we'd finished taking on stores, slept soundly for several quiet nights and waited for a gale system to pass, we set sail with a jib borrowed from David and Doreen on *Swan II*. Within two hours of lifting our anchor to tack out of the anchorage and through twelve miles of coral-strewn waters to reach open water my piloting again proved in error. The errors compounded until we had to spin 180 degrees in order to reach clear of an area strewn with coral heads. I was baffled, as this was a space where, according to my calculations, we should have found deep clear water. Larry's trust in my piloting was shattered, and so was mine. By scouring

Even if I didn't enjoy strumming, I'd probably want to carry a guitar on board as many of our guests pick it up and turn quiet visits into a party. This is what happened as we waited for the weather to improve before we departed from Nuku'alofa.

the horizon with binoculars, we found the correct channel markers and worked clear. I was silently castigating myself, wondering if I was competent enough to be a sailor, trying to find excuses for my errors.

For two hours after we'd come within a few feet of hitting those coral heads I tried to decide what to say to Larry, how to apologize, how to regain his confidence. Then a simple difference of opinion sparked an argument that solved my problem.

There is a dangerous reef two miles west of Tongatapu Island and on a direct route between it and Minerva Reef; this marked our turning point on the way to New Zealand's Bay of Islands. Duff Reef breaks in a spectacular swelter of waves that can be seen for miles, even during the calmest weather. We were broad-reaching with the spinnaker set to a very light breeze on a course I'd plotted to give us a mile and a half clearance from Duff Reef.

I was below making lunch when Larry called, "Let's jibe; we're too close to the reef. It's less than a mile off and I feel like we're getting set onto it."

I came out to help and said, "It looks more like two miles away to me."

Like any couple, we have tended to take on jobs we most enjoy doing and I really liked the paperwork of coastal navigation and prided myself in doing a careful and concise job. But as I remembered the problems of the past week, instead of getting annoyed at my navigation being questioned, I said, "Okay, I'll take some bearings and show you."

My bearings, taken with the same handbearing compass we'd used for seven years of yacht delivery and the past two years of cruising, showed the reef to be over two miles south of us.

But Larry was still adamant. "That reef is too damn close."

He became obstinate – and thank goodness he did.

"You watch the main compass and tell me the reading when I line the land up on the back stay. Then ***I'll*** go down and plot our position!"

His bearings were each ten degrees different from mine. We were only 1¼ miles from that boiling cauldron of breaking waves: a minimally safe distance.

Then, the proverbial light began to come on. I went below and brought the handbearing compass out on deck. As Larry called the readings from our main compass, I sighted along the straight edge of our cabin sides, then along the cabin back, and finally right down the centerline of *Taleisin*. Every reading was off by at least seven to ten degrees.

I got out the charts we'd used since we left the Vava'u group. Every problem we'd encountered had been caused by that handbearing compass deviation. I'd faithfully taken bearings on various small islands when we left Nomuka for the 60-mile reach south to Tongatapu in gale-force winds. Each fix had shown us being set eastward. When I recomputed these fixes using my new information I saw we'd not been set at all – we should have been holding a course ten degrees closer to the wind. Had this been an error in the opposite direction, we could have sailed right into an area of unmarked shoals and breakers. We'd used that handbearing compass to try to locate the leading lights inside the huge bay of Nuku'alofa. And because of the error, we'd been looking for them in the wrong places that jinx-ridden night.

When I showed him the reasons for each of our navigation errors, Larry asked, "Didn't we use that handbearing compass to come into Santa Maria bay at night last year?"

We began listing the times we'd depended on bearings we'd taken as we cruised along Mexico's Baja California coast, yet we could remember no navigational surprises in Mexico. Then, as we talked of the last year of sailing, we realized we hadn't had the handbearing compass out of its box for ten months – not until we headed south from Vava'u. Though we'd swung our main compass twice yearly during the previous two years of sea trials and cruising, we'd never checked the handbearing compass against fixed landmarks.

"Maybe it's age, maybe the tropical heat. But the handbearing compass is definitely wrong," I said, "And the worst thing is, there doesn't seem to be any logic to the deviation of the readings. Sometimes they are off to the east, sometimes to the west."

"So put the darned thing away and we'll just use the main compass, buy a new handbearing compass when we get to New Zealand," Larry said.[2] "Let's forget anything but enjoying these light winds. Probably won't last."

And once clear of Duff Reef, with the spinnaker set to a ten-knot breeze, the heavy mood of the previous week lifted, and my doubts about my piloting skills slowly began to melt away.

The passage south from Tonga or Fiji towards New Zealand is one that causes a certain amount of concern for most voyagers and downright worry among those for whom this is their first foray into higher latitudes along the so-called "Milk Run." After thousands of miles of sailing with warm, following winds, there is a strong chance this passage will throw up brisk headwinds along with potentially stormy frontal systems in the approaches to New Zealand. Facing sailors at the end of many months of favorable tradewind sailing is the reality of heading into colder water and colder weather. Further, the passage requires ten or twelve days (or more) at sea, after months of island hopping that includes only a few overnight sails as most of the anchorages are just a daysail apart.

I had prepared for the colder and wetter conditions by moving our heavier clothing to the front of the storage lockers and getting out our

2 In New Zealand, we visited a compass specialist. He asked, "Is your compass compensated for the southern hemisphere?"

I thought he was joking. But then he showed me several brand name compasses, each labeled: *Compensated for southern hemisphere*. He also showed me the book, *Notes on Compass Work* by Kemp and Young, which states, ***"Angle of Dip*** – at positions other than on the magnetic equator, a freely suspended magnetized needle will lie in the plane of the magnetic meridian but will be inclined at an angle to the horizontal. This angle is known as the angle of dip and is said to be positive in the northern hemisphere where the north end of the needle is inclined downwards and negative in the southern hemisphere where the north end of the needle is inclined upwards."

When we checked our Danforth Constellation main compass, which has a card suspended in a large bowl, we noticed the card was tilted almost ten degrees to the north. This tilt, or "dip" as it is called, is not a problem in a bulkhead mounted compass which has a globe-like bowl because the card can still swing freely. But inside a flat handbearing compass, and in some binnacle mounted compass's the card bottoms out at the edges and starts to drag. To make the compass card move freely, you can try tilting the compass, but then it becomes difficult to read and the bearings can still be inaccurate.

To ensure each of us gets sufficient sleep, we start our night watches promptly at 2000 hours. We prefer a three-hour watch system. We carry extra bed pillows, which we use as padding between the sleeper and the hull of the boat.

Since it takes fourteen to sixteen hours to ensure we each get sufficient sleep, some of this sleep time is during daylight hours. We rig this curtain to cut out the light and ensure the off-watch can continue to sleep soundly.

I am always concerned when I hear the rattle of the tin can full of nuts and bolts that serves as a fish alarm. Too often the fish that has grabbed our line is huge. Fortunately, this mahi mahi, caught a day out of Nuku'alofa, was just the right size.

second set of foul weather gear. Larry had checked over our kerosene heating stove, trimming the wick and then lighting it to be sure it would warm us without filling the cabin with black smoke. We'd added extra lashings to secure Larry's very heavy tool boxes, put the storm staysail and para-anchor where they could easily be reached and bent the storm trysail onto the special track that ran from deck level up alongside the mainsail track. Then Larry had folded it into its quick opening sausage-like bag along the cabin top. And I'd moved the ingredients for several simple-to-prepare meals and treats into the settee locker so that, in spite of any rough going we might encounter, we could easily get something to eat. Together we'd spent time studying the British Admiralty publication, *Ocean Passages for the World*, along with the US NOAA *Pilot Charts* not only for the month of November when we were actually heading off, but for October and December to get a clear picture of the average weather patterns, and the areas where the risk of gales was higher. Then we'd laid out a proposed course, west-southwest to take us just north of the Minerva Reefs, then southwest, staying just above 30 degrees south latitude until we were in the same longitude as the northern tip of New Zealand, then due south. Though it added about 100 miles to our voyage, this route would keep us on the edge of the tradewinds where, with luck, we'd have consistent easterly breezes and, once we turned south, if the southwesterly winds that tend to prevail near New Zealand filled in, instead of having to beat to windward, we could lay into our destination, the Bay of Islands, on a beam reach.

The last-minute rush of provisioning then stowing the dinghy on deck and getting underway, plus the day's compass-induced drama, left us both feeling exhausted that first night out. Even though the wind still held light and steady, I wasn't comfortable carrying the spinnaker while I was alone on watch. So, after Larry finished lighting the kerosene running lights and I cleaned up the galley, we worked together dousing the spinnaker and setting the nylon drifter in its place. Though the loss of sail area cut her speed down a bit, *Taleisin* still moved smoothly across a slowly undulating sea, rippled by the gentle breeze, at three knots.

At 2000 hours Larry climbed into the pilot berth and we started our formal watch pattern. I fought to keep my eyes open and my mind alert as I stood that first watch. I fell instantly asleep when I climbed into the body-warmed bunk three hours later. Two watches later when Larry greeted me with a warm smile, a hot cup of tea and plate of chocolate cookies (what others may consider a lousy breakfast, but one I have survived on for several decades), I felt amazingly refreshed even though the motion of the boat told me things outside were changing.

"Pretty big swell rolling in from the southeast," Larry said when I joined him on the sun-warmed deck. "I dropped the mainsail so it wouldn't slat and wake you. Sheeted the drifter in to cut down the rolling."

Taleisin was making a scant knot through the water.

"Feels good to be at sea again," I said.

"Couldn't agree more," Larry replied. "No coral heads to worry about, no anchors threatening to drag."

"And no need to rush around trying to buy things on my list from shops that probably don't have what I want," I added. "Funny how I seem to make do with whatever we have on board once we actually set off. Wonder what kind of weather is coming at us with this swell?"

Of all the experiences offered by our voyaging life, the one both Larry and I rank right near the top of our favorite's list is that time when we fall completely into the rhythm of being at sea, far from land, well beyond the range of our hand-held VHF, with no outside contact unless we decide to listen to something other than the WWV time ticks and weather updates on our shortwave radio receiver. There is nothing on shore that can equal this interval when all that matters, all that seems to exist, is the constellation of the two of us, the boat and the sea around us. I love the feeling that seems to happen a few days into any passage when I realize absolutely no one knows where we are, and nobody cares. Even when the sailing is difficult, as it definitely was for several days after we left Nuku'alofa, I have rarely been eager for a passage to end.

During the first days of our voyage away from the tropics, we both had to work hard to keep *Taleisin* moving efficiently. Calms lasting two or three hours were interspersed with brisk headwinds that lasted a half day, only to slowly lift us back onto course then fade away. Squalls seemed to blow up just as one or the other of us had fallen soundly asleep during our off watch.

So I wasn't surprised when, on our third day out, Larry finished laying his afternoon position on our passage chart and said, "Do you really want to stop and anchor at Minerva Reef? We should alter our course now so we make our approach from the north."

"Don't you want to chase after some lobster?" I countered. "I hear the diving is amazing. And I think four or five of our friends are going to try

Motukokako Island, better known as Hole in the Rock Island, marks the entrance to New Zealand's Bay of Islands.

to rendezvous there."

"Done a lot of good diving. Didn't promise anyone we'd actually meet them there. We'll catch up with most of them in New Zealand in a few weeks, or a year from now when we get to Australia. After the hurricane season we can sail back here if you want, or head to some other atolls – but right now I'm content to stay at sea."

For another three days the fickle weather kept us truly "working the ship" with winds changing every few hours. We'd be beam reaching under all three working sails when a squall would roar down on us to leave *Taleisin* bucking directly into a lumpy sea. Sometimes we could just lay our westerly course close-hauled, then a fading wind would leave us becalmed on an almost flat sea for five or six hours, only to be followed by a 20-knot headwind. Though both of us occasionally grumbled about the fickle weather, Larry, who has slightly hermit-like tendencies, was in his element: at sea, working to get the best possible speed out of the boat, making adjustments to the sails and windvane. And even if on land I am totally gregarious, I too was content, filling any spare time writing notes for stories that seem to find their way into my mind far more easily when we are at sea.

Everything on board seemed to be just as it should be. My fresh food stocks were holding up well; Larry had caught a large mahi mahi two days out of Nuku'alofa and the last big fillet was keeping well on ice. We were both well rested and each day's noon sight crossed neatly with the morning sight to show that, in spite of the weather, we were at least 100 miles closer to our destination.

A thick covering of cloud had been hiding the full moon on our seventh night at sea. It was 0330 when I finished hauling up then sheeting in the nylon drifter to keep *Taleisin* moving on the fitful breeze that had filled in from the southeast. Then I headed back to the cockpit to check our course. Due west, read the compass – just as we wanted. I looked ahead towards the horizon. Instead of the dull dark grey/black monotone I'd seen just minutes before, a bright orange line now marked the margin between sea and sky. Slowly the orange margin grew wider, and as I watched, the center turned into the round orb of the moon. The lower edge of the glowing moon seemed to flatten then spread like a melting ball of ice cream. I sat mesmerized as the moon sank below the horizon, the orange glow dimmed and the sky to the west began to fill with stars.

Then I noticed the movement of the clouds. For the first time in many months, instead of moving from the east, they began to move from the west, almost like a curtain, revealing clear skies head. An hour later the skies around us were completely cloud-free. Directly overhead the Milky Way seemed to be at its very brightest, and the four stars of the Southern Cross sparkled distinctly, well above the horizon on our port beam.

"We've reached the turning point," Larry announced at noon. "Course is now 198 degrees, directly towards the Southern Cross, straight for New Zealand. We'll probably lose this easterly wind pretty soon, hit some headwinds. But maybe then things will steady out for a bit. Be nice to have a day when we don't have to make a half dozen sail changes."

We'd had to drop the drifter earlier in the day and now were moving across a bumpy sea, close-hauled with the borrowed jib and mainsail set to an eighteen-knot southeasterly. Over the next few hours, the wind slowly backed to the northeast and began to lighten; the seas began to flatten out. By morning when Larry asked me to come on deck and help him set the spinnaker, there was only a small hint of a southerly swell undulating across a lightly rippling sea under absolutely clear skies. Unfortunately, the slight swell was just enough to make the mainsail slat, as the light following breeze didn't have the power to still it. Larry lowered the sail but left it lying loose in the lazy jacks and ready to re-hoist quickly should we need it to blanket the spinnaker in the case of a quick and necessary dousing.

And then it began, the memory maker. For four days we sailed smoothly onward at a sedate 4.5 knots, mainsail flaked on the boom, spinnaker set day and night, windvane in perfect control even though there was barely enough breeze to make me want to tie back my unruly mane of hair. The barometer absolutely steady, the skies clear, the sea unchanging.

Hour after hour that big blue and white sail pulled us onward. To me this was sailing at its very best; life was easy on board, my only concern being that nothing could be or stay this good. Every two hours I tapped the barometer, watching for a sign of change.

Every change of watch I said, "Do you think this will last?"

And each time I did Larry replied, "Stop worrying. Just relax and enjoy it."

The fair light winds did last, our spinnaker pulling us right to the entrance of the Bay of Islands. It was with a sense of melancholy that I hoisted the mainsail in preparation for the reach across the bay and up the river estuary leading to Opua while Larry unlashed the anchor.

"Best sailing ever," I smiled.

"Except for you constantly worrying the weather would change, the last few days were almost perfect," Larry teased. Then he added, "Almost hate for it to end. But when we get the anchor down we can say *Taleisin* took us elegantly and successfully across the whole Pacific."

As I searched out our ship's documents and our passports, I thought about how, unlike most other aspects of life, passage-making has a definite beginning, a definite end. Each safe landfall leaves you with a sense of accomplishment. So though I was reluctant to give up the simplicity of our daily routine, the intimacy that formed between the two of us when we were at sea, I looked forward to setting our anchor, completing the official clearance papers, then heading ashore for our traditional end-of-a-voyage dinner. I knew we'd search out a café that would allow us a perfect view across the water to where *Taleisin* lay at anchor. Then we'd raise a toast to the sturdy little vessel that had brought us to this highly satisfying conclusion and, with luck, would soon carry us towards another beginning.

Looking forward from the companion way, this is Taleisin's *main cabin with a settee both port and starboard, pilot berths above each settee, a chart table to starboard and the galley to port. Note the stove is mounted on the main bulkhead for safety reasons, which are explained in* The Care and Feeding of Sailing Crew. *On the mast is our coffee grinder.*

EPILOGUE

It was a letter that actually brought us to New Zealand. When we set sail from Mexico we'd had only one definite goal: to follow a route different than the one we'd taken on *Seraffyn.* There were dozens of new destinations we hoped to reach some day, places like Tasmania, Africa, Argentina and eventually some of the European countries we'd missed the first time around. New Zealand had not actually been one of these. But as we ventured south and west through Polynesia, we knew we had to get *Taleisin* safely south or north of the cyclone belt before the onset of the cyclone season in December. North offered dozens of interesting island groups – the Solomon Islands, Vanuatu, the Philippines. South could only be New Zealand or Australia. We carried charts for several of these destinations, but we were biased towards Australia because we had kept up a long-running correspondence with a sailor from north of Brisbane whom we'd met many years before in the Azores.

Then, during our stay in Papeete, we'd received a letter from Eric and Susan Hiscock suggesting we rendezvous in New Zealand's Bay of Islands.

We'd first come to know the Hiscocks through Eric's books, books Larry had read in the school library when he should have been studying, books we devoured as we outfitted *Seraffyn* for our first foray into cruising under sail. Together the Hiscocks had set sail from the south of England on

30-foot *Wanderer III* when small boat cruising was a rarity. Eventually they voyaged three-and-a-half times around the world. Seamanship, competency – these were the words to best describe Eric's attitude towards voyaging.

It was 1970, just five months into our voyaging life, when we were hired to deliver a 48-foot trawler from Baja California in Mexico north to San Diego, that we first met Eric and Susan in person. We arrived at the guest dock of the San Diego Yacht Club where the owner was to take charge of the trawler. There, secured just ahead of us on the dock, was *Wanderer IV*, the Hiscocks' current vessel. Though Eric was known for his British reserve and reticence, he generously opened his boat to these two brash, enthusiastic young voyagers. Over the next several years as we met in various ports around the world, we slowly became friends. But a joke grew between us, Eric and Susan both teasing us about our mythical "small sailboat." The reason? Each time we happened to cross paths, Larry and I were delivering someone else's boat. One time it was a 40-foot racing sailboat, then it was a 55-foot heavy displacement (and to our eyes very ugly) ketch, then a bulky 45-footer bound for a charter fleet. We'd have a few hours to catch up with each other before Larry and I had to move on to ensure we got the boat to its owner at the agreed time. But it was in letters that our friendship flourished: Susan writing of sailing friends we should watch for who might be cruising near where we were headed; Eric generously – and with a very dry sense of humor – offering his advice on articles I'd share before sending them to an editor. A comment I'll never forget: "You must stop dropping so many anchors. Maybe you could set them instead."

The letter we received in Papeete suggested that Eric and Susan would set sail from Australia to meet us if we were willing to sail to New Zealand, where we could, for once, have more than a day or two to share each other's company. The letter had a post script: "If you, like us, should want an eventual home base which suits sailing wanderers, it would pay to consider that gentle and amenable country."

We arrived in New Zealand's Bay of Islands, eager to catch up with two people who had been instrumental in inspiring the dream of cruising in Larry's young racing sailor's mind. Intrigued by Eric's and Susan's interest in making New Zealand a home base after more than 30 years of wandering, we decided to spend the next five or six months exploring these waters to learn out why the Hiscocks found them so inviting, before sailing towards Australia's Great Barrier Reef once the cyclone season had passed. A few days after Eric and Susan sailed in to anchor alongside us after their seventh crossing of the Tasman sea, at ages 77 and 74, respectively, we were together on board *Wanderer V*, looking over charts of their favorite New Zealand destinations.

"Since both of us are headed towards Auckland after we leave the Bay of Islands," Eric stated, "I suggest we get together again in North Cove at Kawau Island. It is right on our route and is a perfectly protected anchorage."

This was just the first of many small incidents that delayed our onward voyage to Australia's Great Barrier Reef by almost three years – and unexpectedly led to us finding a home.

Our anchor windlass stopped working near Opua, again. As usual, when Larry disassembled the windlass, he found the pall return springs had broken – again. With infinite patience, he cut miniature toggles from a piece of the bronze scrap we carried on board. With the toggle providing more flexibility in the system, the springs never again failed.

Replacing the jib we'd lost overboard near Nuku'alofa was an interesting introduction to New Zealanders' attitude to what could be called the work/life balance. We contacted North Sails and emphasized the importance of getting a new sail as soon as possible.

"It is less than two weeks until Christmas holidays start," the sailmaker stated. "We close the loft so everyone can enjoy the holidays then go on summer holiday with their families. Don't reopen until third week in January." He then went on to further explain in a congenial manner, "We don't work overtime or Saturdays and Sundays at this time of the year; weather is too good and folks want time with their families. If you need your sail before February, you'd better come down here and help us build it."

We were on a bus to Auckland within the week. We returned four days later with a new sail.

While we were in Auckland, I found a music store and purchased a dozen sets of guitar strings which I knew were almost impossible to buy in Tonga, plus a roll of the thin wire used for the easily broken 6th or E string, then sent this, along with a few other gifts, to the Hausia family at Pangai Motu, Vava'u. I included a letter in which I mentioned I was excited to learn my parents would be flying down to New Zealand for six weeks to visit us. An express letter arrived soon after, postmarked Tonga. I was surprised as the cost of express postage was equal to a whole day's taxi driving earnings for Ponove.

"My mother says you are part of our family," the letter read. "So your parents are our parents too. They must come and stay with us."

Molokeini Tollemach, whom I first met at Niuatoputapu.

I shared this message the next time I was on the telephone with Mom.

"Of course we'll go visit them too. I'll change my airline ticket so we can go there in the middle of our visit," she wrote back. "What shall I bring along as gifts for the family?"

I warned her it wasn't easy to get to Pangai Motu – that, after flying from Auckland to Nuku'alofa, she would have to spend two days on a rather primitive ferry to get to Vava'u, and that the Hausia family home was unsophisticated, with no indoor plumbing and none of the modern accoutrements my parents were accustomed to.

My 68-year-old mother replied, "And who taught you to camp?"

My parents spent two weeks of their six-week South Seas sojourn in Tonga, returning to New Zealand to tell us how the whole family and half the villagers from Pangai Motu were at the ferry landing in Neiafu

Lini Hausia, our Tongan god-daughter, with her daughter Vashaili.

to greet them. They were escorted to the plantation where a completely new cottage had been woven for them, the palm frond walls still green and sweet-smelling. The family had borrowed a proper bed from the local priest so my parents would not have to sleep on floor mats. They were treated like treasured guests and only reluctantly allowed to help with harvesting copra.

"Best holiday in my whole life," my father told me. "And you are going to be god-parents. Lisa says the only reason she is pregnant again is because of the wine she drank on your boat, so she is going to name the baby Linlarry if it is a girl, Larrylin if it is a boy."

Several months later a cruising boat came to anchor near us in New Zealand. "We have gifts for you from your Tongan family and photos of your god-daughter too," we were informed.

Through the years I have kept contact with Linlarry (pronounced Leen–lauree), who goes by the name of Lin. She has three handsome children and, with her Australian partner Greg Edwards, now runs a well-regarded cafe on the Gold Coast in Australia.

Twenty-three years after our first sojourn in Tonga, we again voyaged through the Pacific, headed towards our home base in New Zealand after completing a second circumnavigation. We sailed in to Niuatoputapu be greeted by Molokeini, who married a New Zealand cruising sailor and, by coincidence, had just returned to the island from her New Zealand home with her ten- and twelve-year-old sons for a long visit with her family. Our reunion was magical, with Molokeini (Keini for short, pronounced Kay-nee) immediately taking my hand and leading me as she had all those years before to greet family and friends.

Keini returned to New Zealand, and so did we. Our friendship blossomed. Keini and her family often spend time with us here at *Mickey Mouse Marine*, the small boatyard and home Larry and I developed on Kawau Island. We use her home as our base when we head into the city.

As I sit at my desk in the office Larry built for me, a tiny but elegant cedar and glass jewel box-like structure which lies halfway between the boatshed and our lovely small wooden house (he built those too), I look out across the waters of this cove to where *Felicity*, our fifteen-foot Herreshoff sloop sits waiting to head out for a bit of sailing and realize our Tongan family's prophecy came true: we now have not only a home, but family close by to care for us.

Taleisin *next to the boat shop at our home on Kawau Island, New Zealand.*

Shipwrecks like this are often the first thing you spot when you approach remote atolls. This one lies a few miles to the east of the entrance of Suwarrow.

One of the pleasures of tropical cruising: diving overboard dressed in nothing but suntan lotion. I carried the spear gun to ward off the often curious but relatively harmless tiny sharks that swam along the edges of this reef.

APPENDIX I

CORAL REEFING CRUISING: THE SAILOR'S VENUS FLYTRAP

This appendix is adapted from an article originally written for SAIL *magazine just after we had completed the voyage described in* Taleisin's Tales, *from Southern California, through the South Pacific and down to New Zealand. It was updated after a third voyage through the Pacific, on a slightly different route in 2009 and used as a chapter in our book,* The Capable Cruiser. *I include it here in condensed form because the stories I tell in* Taleisin's Tales *may not give people a balanced view of both the pleasures and potential challenges of cruising along what is commonly called The "* Milk Run,*" a name that implies sailing along this route is easy.*

Anchorage Island, Suwarrow, the refuge where New Zealand hermit and author, Tom Neal, found solitude and contentment for sixteen years. The nearest inhabited land lay 400 miles away. The quiet anchorage we'd found here was like a balm after a stormy passage from Bora Bora. Like so many voyagers who have stopped here, I too wanted to fall in love with this place – a place that is unique because the only way you can reach it is to sail across an ocean.

We spent the afternoon after we arrived ashore on Direction Island. As Larry and I rowed past the seven other yachts lying between us and *Taleisin*, we commented on the wish we shared with every other person we met at Suwarrow: that we'd find ourselves completely alone in this romantic spot. Yet despite the apparent "crowd" of boats, here was a truly international group of sailors – French, American, German, Australian, Belgian. Each had a special story to share. Each added to the special flavor of this place and made me want to linger for a long time.

It wasn't until a few days later when the incessant 22- to 28-knot easterly trade winds increased just a bit and began to swing slightly to the south that Suwarrow's charm turned just a bit frightening. Like so many South Pacific anchorages, this one could turn out to be a watery version of the flower called the Venus Flytrap. A 30-degree wind shift, a sudden squall from the south – these could, and often did, turn this bit of heaven into a sailor's image of hell.

It was Larry who finally crystallized our thinking about the voyaging we'd been doing since we'd left Mexico. "Some people call this route from the Marquesas through the Tuamotos and Societies then eastward the 'Milk Run.' But I don't agree. The passage-making may be easy; it's almost all downhill. The weather is warm, the water is warm; even we can catch fish here."

I nodded in agreement; I knew where he was going with this.

"But as soon as you get near the atolls and islands, the demands on your seamanship and navigation is tougher than any place we've been," he continued. "The reefs, the currents, the lack of navigational aids, the poor anchorages – cruising down here means constant concern. Then, if you find you have to go home for some reason, all of that running downwind means you have to beat back against those same strong tradewinds. It reminds me of what our old cruising friend Gordon Yates used to say: 'If you aren't afraid you just don't know the facts.'"

Approaching an Atoll

Coral reefs have always made experienced sailors nervous. Even the advent of modern electronic navigational equipment hasn't kept commercial ships off the sheer cliff a coral reef presents to the unwary. There is no shoaling, no gradual change in the wave patterns as you approach most of these atolls since they leap straight up from depths of 2,000 feet or more. Worse yet, most reefs are only visible at low tide unless a sandy motu or island has formed and trees have grown. If there are trees, on a clear day, the watchful sailor could spot the tops of tall palms from six or eight miles off. Otherwise it is hard to see a coral reef from a mile away. At night you have no chance at all until you are right in the surf line. Add to this the fact that normal ocean currents increase their velocity and often change their direction close to coral reefs and you'll understand why the *British South Pacific Sailing Directions* devotes several pages to a section on navigation among coral reefs.

We had been reluctant to sail among the Tuamotos, an archipelago of dozens of coral atolls with a name that translates to "Dangerous Islands." Several professional delivery skippers we knew had come to grief there, even on boats with powerful engines. We'd planned a route to take us from the high volcanic islands of the Marquesas to the 3,000-foot volcano of Tahiti, clearing these atolls by 50 to 60 miles. But then we met Frank Corser, a cruising sailor who'd been seduced fifteen years previously by the lure of the South Pacific and, at the time we arrived in 1985, owned a tiny hotel in Taiohae Bay on Nuku Hiva. Frank had been through the Tuamoto Islands a dozen times under sail. He felt we'd regret passing without visiting at least one of the atolls and he had a seamanlike set of rules for approaching the Tuamotos: Plan a course that will make your approach a beam reach or close-hauled approach and keeps you beam-on to the current. Make your approach from the north and east, so if you don't get good conditions and have fluky winds, squalls or poor navigation fixes, you can reach north and clear the whole island group. Only approach within ten miles of the atoll on sunny days after you have confirmed your position. Don't be too determined to get in.

We took his advice and chose Rangiroa, one of the most northerly atolls, as our first goal. Using our sextant to take both sun shots and star shots, we took care to approach as recommended, from the north. When we were within 70 miles of our landfall, dark began to fall. We made the decision to carry on for a few hours more, and then we and hove to 40 miles out to wait for morning.

When I spotted the tree tops of the northernmost motu two hours before I expected them, I was glad we'd chosen to heave to offshore. We'd been set ten miles towards the reef during that night, the current had been flowing at 1-3⁄4 knots to the southeast where the charts showed a due easterly current of less than a half knot for our area. We were lucky to be far enough out to have time to assess and make a considered decision about our final approach. Others had more harrowing stories to tell. Glen, a New Zealander on a cutter-rigged H28 whom we met later at Rangiroa, had chosen the opposite tack. He'd hove to only ten miles out during that same night and gone below for four hours' sleep. When his alarm clock woke him, he was only a quarter mile from the breakers.

"Only ten minutes more sleep and I'd have hit the reef," he recalled soberly.

Through the Pass

Our first atoll landfall increased our confidence and by the time we approached Suwarrow we'd become comfortable with our routine of keeping an offing until we confirmed our position and could approach in daylight. During this time we'd met dozens of sailors who told us, "If you had GPS (or its precursor, Sat Nav), these reefs wouldn't be any bother at all." We also met several new to cruising people who were changing their plans and forsaking visits to certain reef areas because their chart plotters or GPS weren't working.

Yet as much as these magic little boxes have come to dominate the sailing world, five incidents that occurred as we sailed in these waters reminded us of the warning manufacturers put on each instruction sheet: "This unit is only an aid to navigation." Two cruising boats were damaged when they approached within four miles of the Tuamota reefs after dark using GPS fixes. They hove to and while they waited for daylight the currents did the dirty deed. Another family bumped their boat onto the reef at Ahe when they came into the pass on a GPS fix in spite of squalls and rain. Fortunately their boat hit on the weather side of the pass and suffered little damage. A fourth yacht was gouged badly when the owners used an electronic fix and came into the pass in one of the Cook Islands during a squall, only to hit a piece of coral that projected into the channel.

The fifth case came from the skipper of a large charter boat, who told me he'd been quite upset with his newly repaired GPS when he started it up in Cooks Bay, Mo'orea. His position put him on top of the mountain a mile and a half away. A careful search of his chart showed Mo'orea as being incorrectly plotted. Many of the islands and atolls of the South Pacific are slightly to the east or west of their plotted position since the majority of charts still in use today were drawn before it was possible to determine accurate longitude. A study of the chart notes usually tells you of any error. But if you should miss the small type, your GPS could lure you into trouble. These same errors are, unfortunately, incorporated into many electronic chart programs.

The most worrisome aspect of GPS, in our opinion, is that some sailors have come to regard it as a substitute for the skills and awareness and sense of caution cruisers used to acquire by learning how to navigate using only a sextant and compass.

An extreme example of how this reliance on electronic navigational aids can create a false sense of security was demonstrated in abundance a few nights after we anchored at Suwarrow. It began when a large New Zealand ketch came in to anchor a few hundred yards from us late in the afternoon and we watched as the crew launched an inflatable, loaded a pile of gear into it then zoomed off at high speed towards the atoll pass. It was well after dark when one of us noticed a light on the horizon to the west. The light seemed to be approaching dangerously close to the atoll. Then we saw a swing of green, red then white that showed it was the masthead light of a sailboat. The light continued east and disappeared behind Anchorage Island.

From our view, the sailboat had seemed perilously close to the north-jutting portion of the atoll. Later, we were stunned to see the lights of the sloop coming though the atoll pass in spite of the cloudy, moonless dark, in spite of the surf breaking on the coral heads which divided the main channel.

We watched, stunned, as the sailboat rafted alongside the New Zealand ketch that had arrived earlier that day.

We came to know the whole story the next day, when we helped the professional delivery skipper of the New Zealand ketch try to locate the beacons he'd set to guide his friends in.

"They'd been beating from Samoa into 25-knot tradewinds for six days and really wanted to get a good night's sleep," he told us. "We'd been in radio contact all along. They'd asked on the radio if I'd come out and guide them in and I really couldn't say no over the radio when I knew a lot of other people were listening in. So when I arrived I checked the channel and decided if I set two man overboard lights on bouys as leading marks, then guided them into position using my radar, they could come through the channel and I could then use my anchor light as the last leading mark to guide them past the inner reef."

Larry and I listened intently.

"I had a hand-held VHF in the dinghy, and my crew with the radar was in radio contact with all of us," the skipper continued. "The radar showed the reef and their boat clearly. It was sort of a fun exercise, laying the lights, planning the bearings."

Unfortunately, the current in the atoll entrance dragged one of the man overboard lights and its 150 feet of line and twelve-pound anchor under, and a lot of expensive gear was lost.

The delivery skipper came over for coffee two days later and seemed a bit less sure of his late night piloting. "They really had to trust me to come in like they did," he said. "They also had to trust my radar. When you think about it, they were putting their boat and their lives in the hands of my electronic gear. They cleared ten-foot breakers by only a 100 yards on a dark, windy night."

We too could imagine the adrenalin charge of planning and executing that nighttime entrance. But we agreed with the skipper it had been an unnecessary risk since no one on board the other boat was sick or injured.

"If they'd hove to and waited twelve hours, they could have assumed all the responsibility themselves and come in the next morning with no risk at all," he said as final comment.

Considering Current

One of my main concerns about sailing into the atolls and into the lagoons of the reef-ringed islands of Polynesia had been locating the passes. At places like Rangiroa where the pass was bordered by two sandy islands with distinctive churches as guiding marks, there were no problems, but what of places like Taha'a, where the pass was only a break in the coral fringe and over a mile from the nearest land?

That concern fell quickly by the wayside as we visited a dozen different atolls and lagoons. At first the excellent navigation marks of French Polynesia helped us learn to define reef entrances and built our confidence until by the time we reached unmarked Suwarrow we knew we'd be able to sight a lagoon entrance just by the change in wave patterns, the curling of breakers around the end of each projection of the reef, the smoother backs of the swells that found their way through the reef entrances, the color changes.

Deciding which way the current would be flowing through atoll passes was the hardest problem to solve. Throughout French Polynesia and the mid-Pacific, there is less than a fourteen-inch rise and fall of the tide.

Wave and swell patterns often influenced the amount and direction of the current more than the diurnal tide changes. The size of the lagoon, how much of the fringing reef was bare, how much was covered by motus or land – these, more than tidal changes, determined the amount of water trying to get out through the narrow passes.

The Pacific pilot books list a complicated formula of moonrise combined with tide table data to determine when we would find slack water to sail through the pass into Rangiroa. We arrived off the pass at Tiputa at the correct time (according to the pilot) and we could see spectacular tidal overfalls accentuated, believe it or not, by dolphins leaping from top to top. The current was clearly running out, at a rate we later learned would attain nine knots. We sailed six miles west towards the second pass at Avatura, remembering the advice of the skipper of a trading schooner we met in the Marquesas: "Moon over head, moon under feet, go!"

We consulted our almanac moonrise and moonset columns, hove to off the pass, saw the overfalls calm and rejoiced as, exactly as predicted, the current stopped flushing out when our almanac showed the moon to be directly under our feet or midway between rise and set.

We sailed into the lagoon on flat calm water.

We watched the overfalls, the flashing current and leaping dolphins in the passes of Rangiroa for several days and learned more about reading the current direction. If the overfalls occurred in the narrowest part of the pass, the water was running in. If the overfalls and rough water were just outside the pass, where the reef fell steeply off into the ocean depths, the current was running out. We rarely saw rough overfalls inside the lagoon, no matter how strong the current.

Although we only experienced a slight bit of current once we were a quarter mile away from the pass inside an atoll, we did find some fierce currents inside the fringing reef of high islands. When we lay at anchor about a mile from the entrance to the reef at Huahine and again five miles from the reef entrance in a secluded safe spot behind Bora Bora, we had as much as four knots of current rushing past. In both cases ferocious winter storms two thousand miles south of us were sending large southeasterly swells crashing across the low-lying southern fringes of the atoll to fill the lagoon. At low water when the fringing reef on the south side of a lagoon was exposed, less water flowed over it into the lagoon and the current slowed a bit. But at high water the crashing waves piled huge amounts of water into the lagoon and it had only one way out, through the nearest, usually relatively narrow reef passage. For four days in each case there was never a slack or incoming current.

It's times like this that you can have trouble getting into lagoons. Conditions like this that have caused many people to wisely choose to by-pass Maupiti Atoll, though, with its interesting archeological remains, it is an interesting waypoint just west of Bora Bora.

Inside the Atoll

Navigating inside coral atolls and lagoons seems deceptively easy. The natural breakwater of the reef calms even the largest swells so that, even on the roughest days, only a small wind chop develops within a mile of the inside edges of the reef. The lack of swell means there is little danger other than to paint and pride even if you do bump a coral head. As all the guides suggest, we tried to sail inside any reefs when the sun was well above the horizon and behind us. We tried polarized sun glasses and used them to help read the varying colors of shallow waters, but we came to realize they were not absolutely necessary to differentiate between the dark blues that meant deep water, the turquoise that spoke of shoaling, the browns that meant coral heads. The visibility inside many reefs on non-stormy days was amazing. I was sometimes shocked when I took soundings on a coral head I felt was only a few feet below our keel, only to find it was 20 feet beneath the surface.

Although it might have been fun to have a set of ratlines and climb to the spreaders to con from there, we found standing on the gooseneck next to the mast let us see far enough ahead to sail among the unchartered coral heads of places like Suwarrow at the modest speeds of two and one half to three knots we found comfortable. It was in the relatively well-marked lagoon of Raiatea where we had our only mishap. Because of the fine new French chart we carried, plus the bouys and navigation marks we could see ahead of us, we relaxed and forgot about keeping a watch from the gooseneck or foredeck. We kept sailing in spite of the sun going behind a cloud. I should also add, we had been challenged to a race against two other cruising boats, so our priorities had shifted somewhat as well. I was skippering and though Larry warned me to give the marks a wide berth – "Remember, coral can grow" – I didn't want to give up an inch and made a straight beeline towards the next mark, leaving the one we were passing only a dozen feet to windward. We clipped a coral head halfway between two marks at two knots. *Taleisin*'s eight and a half tons kept her moving, a hard swing to port got us back onto deep water and two hours' work with a hammer and putty eight months later when we hauled *Taleisin* out of the water in New Zealand covered the signs of our lapse. Meanwhile, the anchorage we found later that day, secluded with fine skin diving, deep firm sand for our anchor to dig in only twelve feet below us and almost 360 degrees of protection, made that momentary heart-in-throat, stomach-upside-down feeling our little prang on the coral left behind seem worthwhile.

Even so, it's a cautionary tale, and one we took to heart.

Anchoring in Coral Heads

Anchoring among the atolls and islands of the South Pacific deserves equal consideration. My memories are of constant concern and only occasional feelings of complete security. From the time we left Mexico until the day we reached New Zealand, we only encountered harbors with 360-degree protection, good holding ground and limited fetch in four places. Everywhere else, we had to settle for 180-degree protection in most places, such as the anchorages we found at Suwarrow. Although the trade winds are amazingly consistent during the non-hurricane season each year, we did experience several sudden shifts from the normal east-northeast or easterly trades to southeast and one time, to south.[1] The switch to south occurs when the ITCZ forms a bulge, and is the one most atoll dwellers find disconcerting because this wind can be quite fresh, while the temperatures drop by about 10°C (18°F). The south winds will sometimes blow for two or three weeks at a time. The storm shutters ready and waiting on all the south-facing walls of Rangiroa's charming Kia Ora resort reminded us of this. While we were there, we never saw them put in place, but they served as a note about the potentially changing weather, even in places that appeared to offer safe, steady anchorages.

About 90 percent of the best anchorages among the atolls of the Tuamotos and Suwarrow are on the northern fringe. A southerly wind turns them into a dangerous lee shore. The far end of the atoll, which is often ten or fifteen miles away, cuts down the ocean swell, but in the anchorages that are used most frequently, a tremendous wind chop can develop in minutes. If this happens in daylight with good visibility it is only an inconvenience: lift anchor and head out to sea or sail to the opposite end of the lagoon and find an anchorage there. But when the wind shifts occur at night (and in the tropics the darkness of night always lasts at least nine hours because of the proximity of the equator) you are

1 During La Niña years, westerly winds are known to fill in for two or three weeks at a time in this area, rendering normal anchorages untenable.

caught in a trap. There are few coral reef areas in Polynesia where you can safely move at night except at the main harbor of Papeete or with local knowledge near a few of the main villages in places like Rangiroa and Bora Bora. Even in daylight, these sudden wind shifts can become more than an inconvenience if you have not found a perfect anchorage because your rode can catch under a coral head's overhanging edges as the boat swings. Unless you can dive or clear your gear, you will have to buoy your anchor cable and let go your gear then sail back later when the weather reverts to normal and retrieve everything.

Choosing a good place to set your anchor is always a problem in coral areas. You have to search hard to find a patch of sand completely clear of coral heads in less than 90 feet of water. So you can either search out the shallow spot, where you lay out your ground tackle and hope the wind holds steady, lay out a stern anchor to keep your rode in the clear area or anchor in deep water, water of 90 to 115 feet, where coral heads are much less common. Any of these choices have major drawbacks.

We found clear sand patches to set our anchor in several places as we cruised through Polynesia. In each case the time we spent searching for these areas was well worthwhile. Instead of the horrid, wrenching, grumbling sound of chain grinding its galvanizing off against coral heads, we only had the swish of chain on sand. To find this peace of mind we often had to anchor a mile or more from villages. But we felt the extra rowing, or the trouble of putting our outboard motor on the dinghy, was worth the effort. Besides, we usually ended up closer to the best skin diving areas this way. We did find a few places where the clean clear areas of sand were a potential trap. In these rare spots, the sand was only a thin layer on top of dead coral. So we usually watched our anchor dig in as we backed the boat down or dove to inspect the depth of the sand and to make sure our anchor was well set.

Our second choice was usually the deep water one. Near the high islands of Polynesia, rivers wash mud into the rifts in the coastline and good coral-free holding ground exists in most waters deeper than 80 feet. I worried about retrieving our gear when we let out 275 feet of chain plus 50 feet of nylon snubber to get a minimum of three-to-one scope in 90 feet of water, yet never, in two dozen anchorages in Polynesia, Tonga or behind Anchorage Island at Suwarrow, did we encounter coral heads in deep water or hear any grinding noises transmitted up our chain.

When we sailed to the seclusion of Bird Island on Suwarrow's far eastern edge, we came up against a third solution, using a stern anchor to line up our gear along a coral-free alley of clear sand. But here one of

Suwarrow's unique problems forced us to try a new anchoring solution. We let *Taleisin* drift back gradually away from her anchor in the largest sand alley we could find. Massive coral heads rose to the surface within 50 yards on either side of us. Another lay 50 yards astern. Larry put on a mask and dove overboard to set our light weight stern anchor by hand so it was well clear of coral heads. He was out of the water before I could turn around. I looked where he pointed and counted over half a dozen sharks–sharks up to six feet long–cruising below our keel.

"I'm not so sure I want to set the stern anchor where I might have to dive to retrieve it," he said. "But we can't let the boat swing or the main chain could catch a coral head and then we'd have a real problem."

We came up with a solution that used our obstacles. Larry rowed our stern anchor out 150 feet and hooked it into a crevasse on the coral head that reached within a foot of the surface astern of us. Then he arranged the chain so it lay across the relatively smooth area on top of the coral head to take any chafe.

Neither chain nor line is perfect solution for anchoring where there are coral heads. Line will chafe through in minutes if a wind shift lays it against coral. So if you use line for your rode, you must buoy it so it stays clear of the bottom. To get the seven-to-one scope required with a line rode for safe holding, you will need to carry several buoys. Chain will let you use slightly less scope, as little as five-to-one in well-protected waters of 20 feet or more. But if you swing and your chain wraps around a coral head so that the chain has absolutely no slack to absorb shocks, a three- or four-foot surge could cause a ten-ton vessel to pitch violently enough to snap the finest $^{3}/_{8}$-inch chain. Letting out more chain will temporarily solve the problem, until this chain also finds the next coral head to snag.[2]One solution found by a sailor trapped in this situation at night was to buoy the extra chain he let out so it couldn't reach the bottom, studded with problematic coral heads. His solution was shown on a note pinned to the bulletin board at Suwarrow, along with handwritten person account of seven hapless voyagers who had all been blown onto the insides of the reef at Suwarrow atoll one August night the year before we arrived. Six of the boats at the atoll that fateful night had been laying on line rodes, two were on chain, when the normal trade winds suddenly turned to the

2 To help conserve coral reefs, always use any mooring which has been provided. (But be sure to inspect the mooring gear before relying too heavily on it. Your boat, your responsibility.) If no mooring is available, try to find coral-free patches for anchoring. If you must anchor among coral heads, use a stern anchor to keep your chain from damaging a wide area of the bottom.

south and freshened just after dark. The chop and waves reached heights of six feet within a few minutes. Every boat broke its anchor rode and was washed ashore except for the one whose owner buoyed his extra chain as he let it out. Five of the boats were eventually salvaged and repaired, and their cruises continued. Two were too badly damaged.

Below these accounts on the Suwarrow notice board, a later visitor to the island atoll had written, "Why didn't they get out to sea?"

We had our chance to ask the same question soon after reading that notice board. It was the hint of a wind shift, a report over WWV[3] saying that a band of southerly squalls was moving slowly closer to our area, plus a slight drop in the barometer from its normal diurnal rise and fall, that sent us scurrying out of the intriguing atoll at Suwarrow. We'd only been there a week. Yet we longed for a 360-degree anchorage, a firm mud bottom and no coral heads where we could relax just for a while after five months of semi-safe anchoring. Pago Pago, 700 miles west, offered just such an anchorage. Six hours after we set sail, the reinforced tradewinds slowly veered until by nightfall we were reefed down for a fast beam reach with the wind due out of the south. Larry and I were seriously concerned about our cruising friends back at the Venus Fly Trap called Suwarrow.

As we rested and re-provisioned in Pago Pago for two weeks, several of the eight cruising boats we'd seen behind Anchorage Island sailed in. Most had stayed only through that initial restless night when the trade winds shifted to the south for the first time in three months and two- to three-foot chop turned their previously dreamlike tropical haven into a restless, nerve-racking threat. The two most novice boat owners stayed three days more because the fear of 30- to 35-knot winds outside the atoll were more frightening than the existing devil inside the lagoon. They arrived in Pago Pago exhausted and frightened and tired of cruising. One of their wives refused to go further and booked a flight for home.

It wasn't until four months after we left Suwarrow and set *Taleisin*'s anchor in the muddy, bottom of a fully protected anchorage, four miles up a river and entirely free of coral heads, that I came to understand completely why so many South Pacific cruisers actually look forward to the hurricane season. Though both of us considered the Tuamotus and Suwarrow to be among the highlights of our South Pacific crossing, the constant vigilance needed to explore among the coral reefs of Polynesia can become unnerving. The chance to find a safe anchorage, to forget

3 WWV is the station that broadcasts time ticks and once hourly Pacific weather warnings on15000kh shortwave.

about your anchor dragging, chafing, grumbling against coral; the chance to give up the concern of coral reef navigation; the chance to reflect on what you've seen – this makes the five- or six-month pause south of the cyclonic storm belt in New Zealand or Australia a welcome relief.

Note: Since 2009 Suwarrow, which is a designated bird preserve and World Heritage Site, has had a permanent caretaker and visitors are limited to a one-week stay unless there are very few boats at anchor. It is more common for there to be a half dozen or even a dozen boats at anchor behind Direction Island than in the past, and you may not sail to other parts of the lagoon without permission. But all of the anchoring and navigation problems discussed in this chapter still hold true. During the 2008 season more than a dozen yachts ended up either abandoned or badly damaged by poor navigation and encounters with reefs. This is described by Grahame and Lynne Brown in an article published by *Blue Water Sailing* in August 2009 called "Anchorage Adventures." It tells of an almost exact reprise of what happened during our visit to Suwarrow.

APPENDIX II

WHAT'S IN A NAME?

Through the years, many people have asked how we came to name our boats. I wrote the following story for SAIL *magazine soon after* Taleisin *was launched to answer that question.*

For two and a half years we listened in frustration as friends, family and magazine editors called the boat that was growing 200 yards from our desert canyon home *Seraffyn II.*

"No," one or the other of us would say. "That's not her name. Would you call your children John, John II, John III?"

This new boat did seem to be like a second child as she grew under our hands, her 21-foot-long keel timber slowly emerging from a solid teak log, her black locust frames flaring like limbs from the glowing bronze floor timbers.

"You should name her *Seraffyn II,*" the late Peggy Slater, a well-known Southern California sailor said. "How else will your old friends recognize you when you sail back into foreign ports?"

Peggy's logic held us for a few moments. Then we each took a glass of wine out to the boatshed and looked at the teak planking which was slowly edging upward towards the sheerline. This boat's profile did remind us of our last little cruising home, the tiny mite that took us so patiently around the world. But there the resemblance ended. Where *Seraffyn* had been pugnacious, tough, almost a bit of a rascal, this new boat already showed the finesse you'd expect now that Larry had combined his ever-growing boatbuilding skills with Lyle Hess' design improvements. The new hull was sleek where *Seraffyn* had been cherubic. The new hull showed proud buoyancy-providing cheeks above her fine bow where *Seraffyn* had the lean look of a young designer's dream.

No, we'd find our old friends another way. This boat needed her own name.

Each week we'd come up with a new one, sometimes serious, sometimes whimsical.

"Let's call her *Maria Elena* like all our Mexican friends call you," Larry suggested one day.

I blushed in appreciation. "Let's call her *Lorena* after your Mexican goddaughter," I countered.

Neither name lasted for more than a few days.

Someone came by and watched Larry fitting the deck strapping into place. "You're building her as carefully as they build Chelsea clocks," the friend said.

And that name caught our fancy. *Chelsea*, easy to say, simple and British like our boat's general appearance. So we wrote the name on a slip of paper and tacked it on our bulletin board to look at, savor, try.

"*Easy Sheets*, that's a name for her," Larry joked one day. "That's what I always call you, Lin. Every time I come out on deck you've eased the sheets."

"*Cariad*, that's a beautiful name," I said as I wrote it on the list under *Chelsea*.

Cariad was the Welsh word for sweetheart, loved one. But Larry felt uncomfortable about naming our boat after the famous 19th century pilot cutter that now sat in ancient splendor at a museum in southern England.

"*Lansing* – we could name it after my favorite square rigged ship. *Lansing* ran the North Atlantic mail line for 30 years and not once was it overdue," Larry said as he added it to our list.

But I wasn't comfortable with that name. Later that evening I re-read a letter we'd received from Sven Lundin in Sweden who expressed my feelings perfectly.

"Choose a simple name, one your boat can grow into and give meaning," he wrote.

And *Lansing* fell by the wayside.

After two years of ministering to this growing, almost living shape it seemed irreverent to call it simply *The Boat*. I found myself falling into the easy trap of saying *Seraffyn II*. That was okay when the hull was out of sight. But if I said it as I sanded and varnished inside her teak planked body, it seemed like I was making a mistake.

We took a weekend trip to San Francisco, *Seraffyn's* new home, and stood on the dock, looking at the little boat that had once been ours, the one that had given us so many thrills and moments of pride. As I stood there I realized there could only be one *Seraffyn*, an entity on her own, waiting, ready to sail on to her next adventure under other hands we hoped would care for her as much as we had.

The quest for a name seemed to grow until every friend wrote suggestions or offered sources. One sent us a dictionary with a name gazette that weighed ten pounds. Another sent us a Welsh-English translation dictionary. Not only was *Seraffyn's* background Welsh, but so was Larry's and the lines of this hull were a development of the Welsh pilot cutters of a century ago. But hours of going over these dictionaries produced some laughter but no name we both liked.

Brion Toss, a softspoken rigger we'd met during our voyaging, wrote to us in a letter that arrived soon after I put the seventh coat of varnish on the boat's transom:

> *Nine years ago I brought home a Newfoundland puppy and set about the task of naming. It is an important, profound task, fraught with peril but extremely satisfying and nourishing if pursued properly.*
>
> *American Indians sweated and fasted for their names – the description of the mature self as opposed to whatever they were tagged with as children.*
>
> *Eskimos tried to find the right name at birth. A sage would attend the labor "calling out" the baby with name after name. When the baby heard its name, out it came.*
>
> *Our own system of indexing seems crude by contrast and of course boats usually fare no better.*
>
> *I brought the dog home and a friend and I sat with him, looking, listening, wondering. We were trying not to be in any hurry, trying not to be cosmic, assuming simply that he had a name and that it could somehow be known. It was a beautiful autumn day. We tried a few names. He panted lightly. We tried a few more. He played with a stick.*
>
> *"Saul," my friend said (she afterwards could not say why), and*

we heard a peculiar resonance, bell-like yet echoing. He trotted over and sat down in front of us.

It is not always like that of course but there is some similar magic, intentional or not, in naming important things. Corresponding vibrations. Mind and nature."

So we waited for the magic, throwing names at the silent hull while we struggled with the endless tasks of fairing up the deck beams, fitting on the cabin sills, scrapping and varnishing the inside of the planking.

The sailing world is very small and sooner or later each voyager seems to have invisible threads leading to others who have known the quiet of calms, the howl of storm winds, the joy of new landfalls. When we happened to meet Tristan Jones one summer day in 1981, we hit it off immediately. His determination, his feeling that obstacles were an excuse for new action, his sheer sense of optimism enthralled us. His Welsh burr, amazing storytelling and quiet ways turned the evening into a bit of the magic usually found only in a secluded anchorage far from shoreside hustle and bustle.

About six months later we heard distressing news. Tristan had lost his leg, not in a sea-going episode, but in the depths of New York where, due to lack of funds, his untreated medical condition flared out of control. We wrote a letter offering our sympathy and half in earnest, half in jest, a piece of teak we had left over after cutting out the stem for our still unnamed boat.

"Larry can rough out a peg leg for you if you want one," I wrote.

Our offer was eagerly accepted and after writing the dimensions we needed to know, Tristan's letter concluded, "What can I do in return?"

Larry got out the hunk of teak he'd offered and set to work gluing on cheeks with waterproof resorcinol adhesive. Then he shaped the peg and couldn't resist more and more finishing touches.

"Ask Tristan to think of a name for us, A Welsh troubadour or minstrel. He's the man who should know."

I couldn't send the beautifully shaped peg leg off without protecting it from the elements it would meet when Tristan again went sailing. So I added five coats of varnish. Then we packed it carefully in foam and shipped it off with a friend who was headed to New York. That same afternoon we received a short simple letter.

June 7th, 1982 New York City
Dear Lin and Larry

Taleisin

Welsh bard from pre-Christian era. He was found in the bull-rushes as a babe and sang the sweetest songs. He sang so sweetly that he cast a spell over the birds so that they flew away in the winter when he slept. He sailed himself over the looking-glass sea and lives in a magic land far away to the west of Ireland. He told the original tales of Mabinogion. Therefore he is the originator of the Tale of Fantasy.

A lovely, honorable name for a boat.
Tristan Jones

We went out to the boatshed and looked at her varnished transom.

"*Taleisin*," Larry said. "Tal-e-sin, a wandering story teller just like *Seraffyn* was."

The golden light of dusk seemed to point out the jobs we'd finished. For the first time I could imagine water lapping against the sides of the rudder that now swung so easily on its shiny bronze pintles. *Taleisin*, a perfect trade, a gift from one sailor to another. Brion had been right; this name did give the correct vibrations. It slid smoothly from our tongues; the boat seemed to respond by changing each day as deck strakes laid more easily into place than they had just the day before.

We called Jay Greer who'd carved the name into *Seraffyn's* transom.

"*Taleisin*," he said, rolling the name slowly. "I love it. It will look elegant carved in classic Roman script, *Taleisin of Victoria*."

Tristan wrote to tell us his peg leg had arrived and would be used and cherished. His letter ended by saying the closest ancient Welsh translation of the name, *Taleisin*, was happy wanderer, lively minstrel or possibly joyful singer.

Once she had a name, it seemed she became a reality. A year after Jay carved it onto the transom and I highlighted his carving with a layer of gold-leaf, *Taleisin* settled slowly into the water to truly live up to the name fate had bestowed upon her.

ACKNOWLEDGEMENTS

Though I have occasionally written stories for various yachting magazines about the sailing adventures we had on *Taleisin*, it has been many years since I wrote a complete cruising narrative like this book. We found, after writing the *Cruising in Seraffyn* series, that practical books seemed to be what everyone wanted from Larry and me: books that directly helped them with their cruising dreams. Statistics prove that nautical how-to books vastly outsell narratives, thus our publisher also encouraged us to put aside pure story-telling. But narratives are rewarding to write, giving me the opportunity to reflect back on the highlights (and occasional lowlights) of life. I discovered this as I wrote (and re-wrote) *Bull Canyon: A Boatbuilder, a Writer and Other Wildlife*, which is a memoir of our time spent building *Taleisin* in an isolated California canyon. Though it is a prequel to *Taleisin's Tales*, and received several heart-warming literary awards, it is not the voyaging narrative that many people would like to read. I know this because over the past few years I have had a surprisingly large number of people come up to me at boat shows or seminars and ask, "When are you going to write another book about your sailing adventures?" They told me *Cruising in Seraffyn* and its sequels encouraged, entertained, even inspired them.

When, a few months ago, I happened to mention in an aside to my Facebook friends that I was settling in to work on *Taleisin's Tales*, the response was immediate and positive. I would like to thank all of those who spurred me on. I hope you enjoy the results.

Leigh Gillard deserves special thanks as a first reader and encourager, as does Mariette Baldwin. I took both of their suggestions seriously. Michelle Elvy, who has worked as Editor on this project, is cruising with her husband and two daughters. She has been more like a mentor than an editor. Her emails, which usually contain interesting personal notes, have arrived from various ports, from Madagascar to Tanzania to Kenya. They have been a special bonus, reminding me that cruising under sail continues to offer an amazing variety of adventures.

Michael Marris and Jill Hetherington here on Kawau Island have been extremely encouraging. Thanks to each of you.

Thanks also to Stephen Horsley, book designer and friend; Tim Murphy, eBook creator; and Jim and Lisa Morehouse and the crew at Paradise Cay Publications, who are more like family than publishing partners. And thanks to the crew at Boat Books New Zealand for help with charts and design ideas.

Larry is listed as co-author of this book. It is obvious that I am the one who actually wrote down the words to create *Taleisin's Tales*. As some of you already know, Larry is by now 76, and Parkinson's disease has taken away many of his abilities. But without him, the tale would have never existed, and through the years we discussed most of the incidents that make up these stories so often, and dissected them so completely, that it is hard for me to know whose words I am actually putting on paper. And as I have read each new chapter to Larry in the writing of this book, he has helped to ensure I include details that matter, and teased whenever my prose went over the top. Larry has been the co-author of an amazing five-decade-long journey, one we are both pleased to share with you.

Now it is over to you, our readers. If, after reading of *Taleisin*'s voyage towards the Southern Cross, you'd like to read more, please let me know by sending a message via Facebook or our website, www.landlpardey.com.

Lin Pardey
At Kawau Island, New Zealand 2016

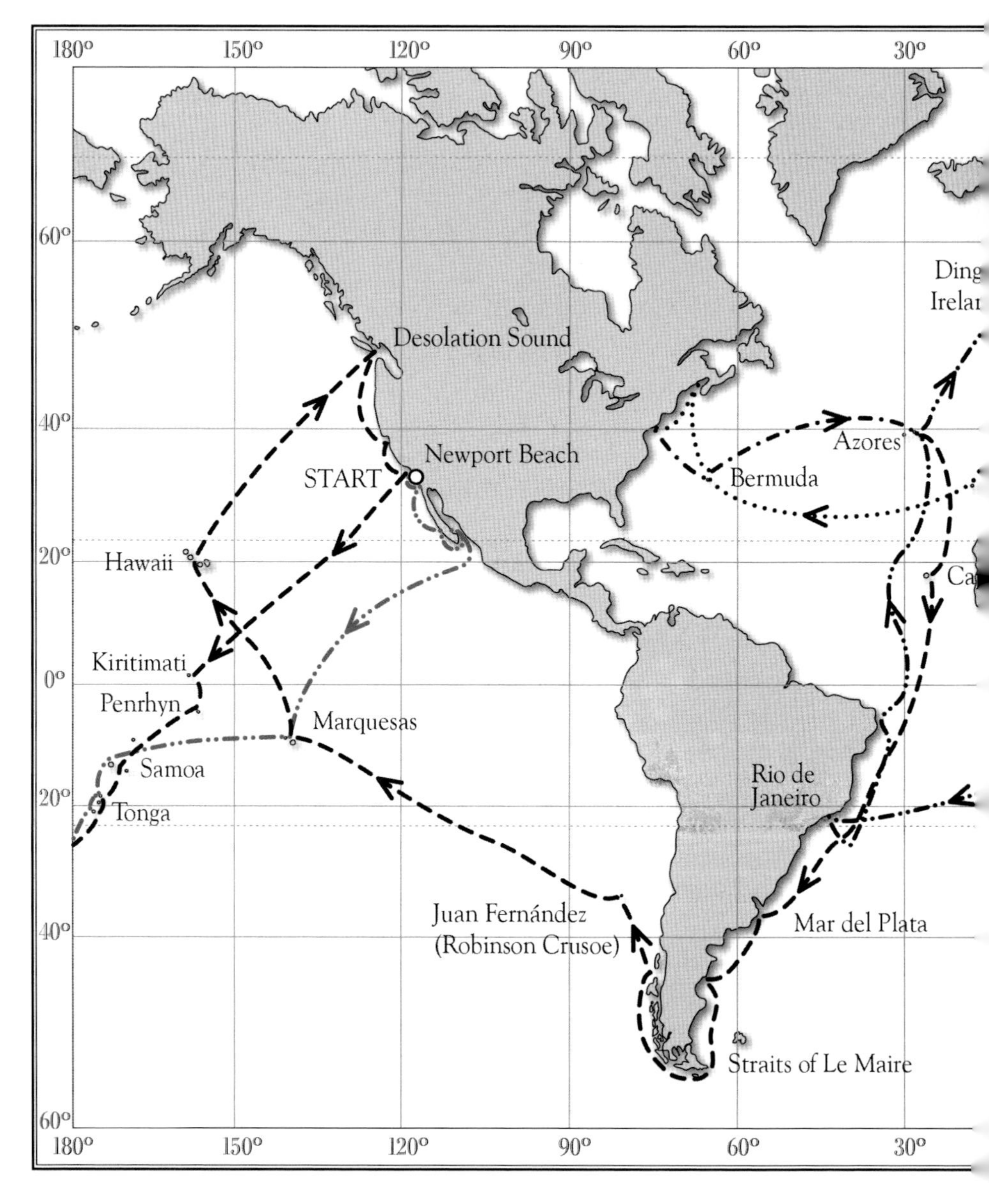

The orange line indicates the portion of her route described in this book
photo by Jacques De Kervor

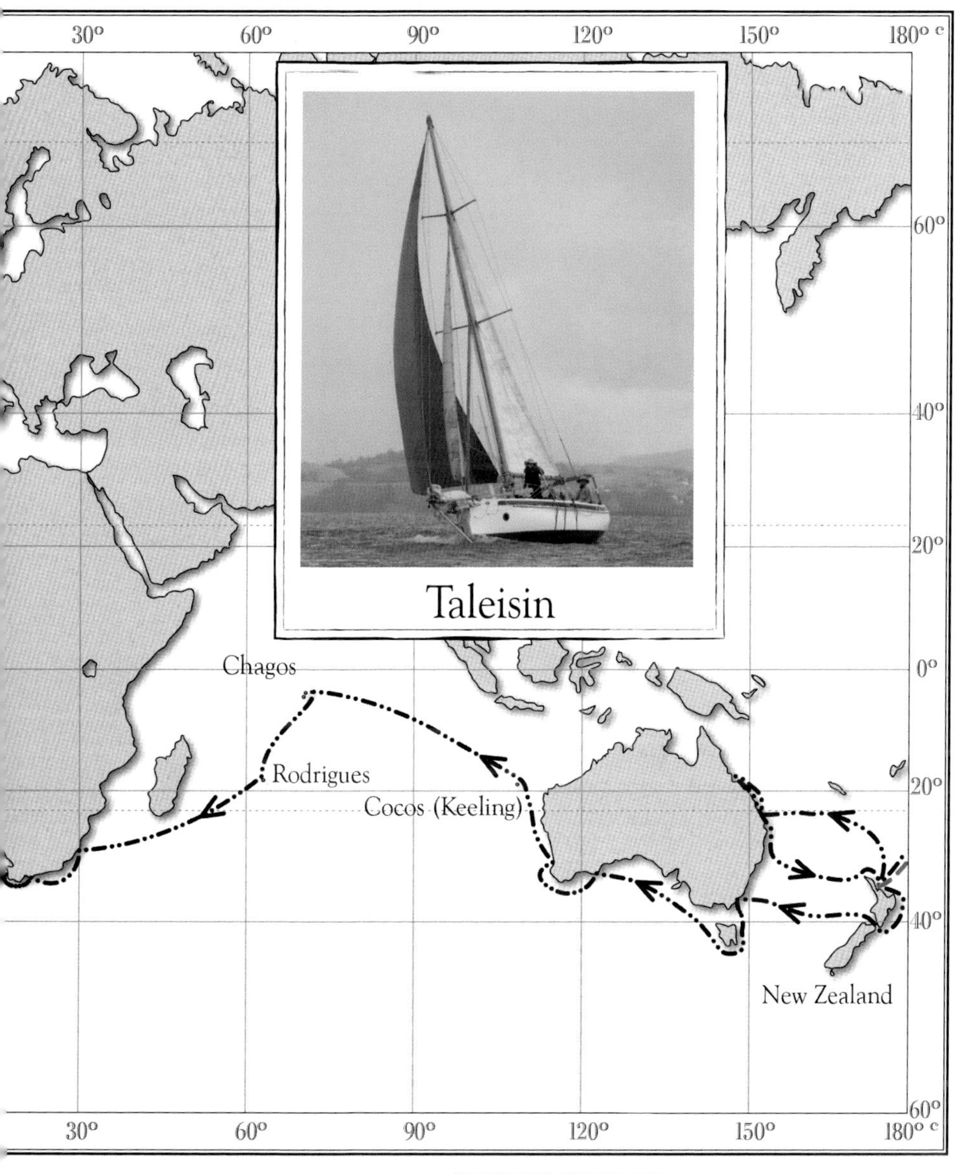

Course of Taleisin 1984 - 2001

Course of Taleisin 2001 - 2010